Queen of the universe

ENCOURAGEMENT FOR MOMS & THEIR WORLD-CHANGING WORK

Susanna Foth Aughtmon

WORTHY
Inspired

Published by Worthy Inspired, an imprint of Worthy Publishing Group, a division of Worthy Media, Inc., One Franklin Park, 6100 Tower Circle, Suite 210, Franklin, TN 37067.

WORTHY is a registered trademark of Worthy Media, Inc.

HELPING PEOPLE EXPERIENCE THE HEART OF GOD

eBook available wherever digital books are sold.

Library of Congress Cataloging-in-Publication Data

Names: Aughtmon, Susanna Foth, 1970- author.
Title: Queen of the universe : encouragement for moms and their
  world-changing work / by Susanna Foth Aughtmon.
Description: Franklin, TN : Worthy Publishing, 2016.
Identifiers: LCCN 2016045249 | ISBN 9781617956690 (tradepaper)
Subjects: LCSH: Mothers—Religious life. | Motherhood—Religious
  aspects—Christianity.
Classification: LCC BV4529.18 .A87 2016 | DDC 248.8/431—dc23
LC record available at https://lccn.loc.gov/2016045249

For foreign and subsidiary rights, contact rights@worthypublishing.com

ISBN: 978-1-61795-669-0

Cover Design: Jay Smith | Juicebox Design

Printed in the United States of America

17 18 19 20 LBM 8 7 6 5 4 3 2 1

For my mom, Ruth,

and

my mother-in-law, Sandy,

(aka Lola)

You have shaped me with your love.

You are the best moms in the universe.

I am thankful you are mine.

Contents

LIZA. What is the matter, boy?

SLIGHTLY. They have all got a mother except me.

LIZA. Is your name Slightly?

SLIGHTLY. Yes'm.

LIZA. Then I am your mother.

SLIGHTLY. How do you know?

LIZA. I feel it in my bones.

J. M. Barrie in *Peter Pan: A Fantasy in Five Acts*

Introduction

THERE ARE REALLY NO WORDS to describe the moment when you first look into the eyes of your child. The mixture of joy and hope and awe is hard to comprehend. The love for this other person is all-encompassing and real. Some of us have always known we wanted to join the league of moms. Others of us stumbled on this vocation by accident. A bunch of us are still in shock that we are actually a mom. (You really are a mom . . . I'm not kidding. . . . It's why you are reading this book right now.) It is a stunning revelation to be sure. Everyone's story of becoming a mother is completely unique, but in each instance, the same thing happens. Your heart is broken open with joy because of the enormous love that you have for this child. Your child.

Maybe your baptism into motherhood was the overwhelming sense of beauty that is linked with the sound of your child's first cries breaking the air. Thankfulness welled up in your chest. Tears streamed down your face. The sight, the scent, the realness of it was too much to take in. It's as if you have caught a small snippet of heaven up in your arms and the glory of it was astounding. Somehow, by the miraculous handiwork of God, you had birthed this small person. Your heart was split wide open with the weight of this tiny one resting against your chest. Love was spilling up and out, filling the room, cocooning you in a place of joy.

Or maybe you have traveled a journey of a thousand miles over multiple years and numerous continents and back again to find your baby. Your journey was rocked with uncertainty and hardship. You never knew that becoming a mother could be so difficult or heart wrenching. But the moment you laid eyes on that little one, whether they were one month or twelve years old, you knew, beyond a shadow of a doubt, this was the child of your heart meant for you and you alone. You are connected by spirit and love. This is your child. You can feel the truth of it down to the very marrow of your bones.

Or maybe you were simply born with a mother's heart. The kind of heart that must hold and nurture and heal. You gather up the lost boys and girls of the world and invite them into your heart, into your life, and into your home. They have come to you in all shapes and sizes, and your love for them mirrors that. You are like a mother bird gathering her chicks under her wings, holding them close and protecting them. There is no child who does not long for or deserve the love of a mother, and you are staking your claim as a stand-in.

However it is that you have arrived at the stage of life called motherhood, you are undeniably, unequivocally, irreversibly . . . changed. Moms are one of God's most lovely creations. Whether your child was born of your body or your heart or both, you are responding to the call of the Father's heart and you are walking out His best plan when you love your child. Being a mom is a high and holy calling. You are the physical embodiment of God's unconditional love. The One who created and ordered the galaxies. The One who sees every child and calls out to them with love.

There is nothing that you will ever do that will be of more value or more importance. Because when you are mirroring the Father's heart of love for His children, you are completing the Great Commission. Whether you realize it or not, with each kiss and hug, with each act of discipline, with each meal cooked and every paycheck brought home, with every prayer prayed and each tear wiped away, you are shaping your child's small heart. You are discipling and teaching and influencing. This is the Small Commission. You are changing the world. One little person at a time.

Whatever phase of mothering you are in, and however many kids you have, I hope this book encourages you—body, soul, and spirit. I hope that you laugh until your sides hurt and grin with joy. I hope that you embrace the beauty of the messy mothering life that you have been gifted with and lean into it. And I really hope that you will see the magnificent mother that you are . . . the one that your heavenly Father created you to be . . . and realize that you are doing good, powerful work every day when you are with your child. May God bless you and surround you with His boundless love and peace on this wild and joyful adventure of growing little (medium-sized and bigger-than-you) people.

To be Queen Elizabeth within a definite area,
deciding sales, banquets, labours, and holidays;
to be Whitely within a certain area,
providing toys, boots, cakes, and books;
to be Aristotle within a certain area,
teaching morals, manners, theology, and hygiene;
I can imagine how this can exhaust the mind,
but I cannot imagine how it could narrow it.
How can it be a large career to tell other people
about the Rule of Three,
and a small career to tell one's own children
about the universe?
How can it be broad to be the same thing to everyone
and narrow to be everything to someone?
No, a woman's function is laborious,
but because it is gigantic, not because it is minute.

G. K. Chesterton

CHAPTER 1

·············

Knowing Who You Are

For we are God's handiwork, created in Christ Jesus to do good works, which God prepared in advance for us to do.

Ephesians 2:10

WHEN QUEEN ELIZABETH ascended the throne in 1952, she was given the auspicious title of Elizabeth the Second, by the Grace of God, of the United Kingdom of Great Britain and Northern Ireland and of Her other Realms and Territories Queen, Head of the Commonwealth, Defender of the Faith. This title was followed by over twenty titles from other various countries and territories that she rules over. She is a truly inspiring woman. What she accomplishes on a daily basis is nothing short of amazing. God Save the Queen!

But in our childhood home on 508 Shurtz Street in Urbana, Illinois, my mom, Ruth Jean Foth, mother of four, wife of Richard, reigned supreme. She was the queen of our suburban kingdom. I didn't know much about Queen Elizabeth, but I knew that my mom was in charge of *everything*. She was the center of our home. The queen of our universe. We revolved around her, held within the gravitational pull of her care. My mom birthed all of us in the span of six years. She says there are large chunks of time that she lost to the fog of young motherhood. Her memory is spotty. But mine is clear on quite a few things.

Mom was always there. She laid herself out as the foundation of our home. Everything she did, she did with us in mind. There were always good meals to nourish us, celebrations with special treats, prayers at bedtime, and the consistent knowledge that we were loved. She told us she loved us, but we knew it already. It was in the air we breathed.

Mom didn't have a clue about what adventure the years held for her after she birthed us. My oldest sister, Erica, could sit quietly and entertain herself for hours with a book. And then there were Jenny, me, and Chris. My mom referred to the three of us younger kids as the "curious" children. You can take "curious" to mean "mostly up to no good." She loved us anyway. She was and is the perfect mom for us.

Becoming a mother will launch you into one of the greatest adventures of your life. Mostly because you have no idea what you are doing. But also because your entire world shifts on its axis. All of your priorities are reordered. Your hopes and dreams, your heart's great longings, and your deepest fears are now filtered through the deep truth that you are caring for a little person. This human being is counting on you to come through for them in every way possible. And you are choosing to rise to the challenge . . . whatever that challenge requires. In that moment of becoming a mother, you are crowned with a great gift and an even greater responsibility.

You are the Queen of the Universe.

Of your universe and theirs. Their world will revolve around yours. Everything, from their spiritual development (this one is of the utmost importance) to their personal hygiene (this one is going to be more difficult than you can possibly imagine), resides within your domain. In the years from your children's birth to their adulthood, you have the great honor of growing and loving them. You get to hold them within the gravitational pull of your care. You get to shape their lives with your goodness and love. There is a great chance that at least one of your children will be "curious." God bless you in advance.

But know this: You are not alone in this endeavor. The One who orders your universe will never leave you or forsake you. He designed this adventure from the get-go. You are His handiwork. He has prepared this good work of motherhood for you in advance. And He has chosen the perfect person to mother this little one whom you love so much. (God never makes mistakes.) That perfect person is you.

· · · · · · · · · · · · · · · · ·

Lord, thank You for this amazing adventure of being a mom.
Thank You for preparing the way before me as I nurture
and love these children. Flood me with Your grace
and wisdom today. Amen.

A Good Queen
Never
Gives Up.

CHAPTER 2

Being a Good Queen

So do not fear, for I am with you; do not be dismayed,
for I am your God. I will strengthen you and help you;
I will uphold you with my righteous right hand.

Isaiah 41:10

AFTER MY COUSIN JESSICA had her first baby, she told me, "You know, there are days . . . multiple days . . . when I never get a shower? And some days I am in my pajamas all day. *All day.*" I was pregnant at the time. I just stared at her. In horror. My fully showered and clothed self didn't know what to say. How could that be? What could possibly keep you from shaving your legs for an entire week? How could watching one tiny person be so much work? Even with all the care that a baby requires, surely there is time enough to put pants on . . . isn't there? *Isn't there?* These were pre-mothering questions.

Of course, now that I have been a mother for fifteen years, I can say with an understanding heart, when you are a mom of a little person or lots of little people or even a few middle-sized people? Putting your pants on is the least of your worries. If you can make it through the day and still find it in yourself to smile before you crash into your bed at night? You are golden. You are a world changer. A life shaper. A molder of the human spirit. Such great work requires brains, guts, and perseverance . . . but not pants. Pajamas will do just fine. Take comfort where you can find it . . . because being a good queen is never easy.

I used to be so judge-y before I had kids. When I would see a mom at the grocery store with her screaming children running free like gazelles on the savannah, I would think, *Sweet mercy, woman! How hard can your job be?* How hard can your job be? For someone who is not living out the dream of motherhood, there is no fathoming how hard it can be.

Being a mom is not just being one thing. It is being all things to one person. Or five people. Depending on how many people you have. Mothering is a compilation of mandatory skills. Not only do you rule your children's universe, you are their teacher, their doctor, their judge, their party planner, their protector, their storyteller, their cook, their adventurer, their defender of the faith, and their maid of all work. The tasks you will accomplish in the mothering years are so many and varied, they can't be listed. You are required to be more than you have ever been before. You will be stretched. And then, stretched some more.

Mothering is not for the faint of heart. It is for the lion-hearted. The brave. The fierce. That mom with the kids swarming in the grocery store? She hasn't lost control. She is braving the wilds of the frozen-foods aisle with small creatures who are on the brink of death almost all the time. She isn't just getting food for dinner. She is teaching manners. She is defining character. She is setting boundaries and saying no to twenty-seven kinds of sugar cereal in the space of a minute. No wonder she looks wild-eyed. She is hyperaware. Buying groceries with kids is like a driver's training exercise—they're filled with chaos at every turn.

Being a good queen is daunting. It is difficult. It is never-ending. And you are just the one to do it. You can be brave. You can be lionhearted and fierce. Because mothering is a love mission. Plain and simple. You love your child exponentially. You are living out this love in a million different ways every day. And the truth is, you were never designed to do it alone. Loving a little person into adulthood is an all-hands-on-deck kind of thing. And the One who loves you most of all is all-in, bolstering your strength, infusing you with courage. He is the Lifter of your head and the Lover of your soul. Lean into His wisdom and grace. He will be with you every single step of the way.

. . . .

Lord, help me to be fearless and brave while I am mothering. Give me strength and courage today to be all that I need to be, and to love this little one exactly the way he needs to be loved. Thank You for being with me. Amen.

My Universe

List the names and birthdays of your child(ren)
and a few words that best describe them.

Name: _____

Birthday: _____

My child is: _____

_____

Name: _____

Birthday: _____

My child is: _____

_____

Name: _____

Birthday: _____

My child is: _____

_____

Name: _____

Birthday: _____

My child is: _____

_____

_____

Prayer for My Universe

Write a short prayer for your child(ren).

Raising a kid
is part *joy*
and part
guerilla warfare.

Ed Asner

CHAPTER 3

Your Gigantic Job

He gives strength to the weary
and increases the power of the weak.

Isaiah 40:29

I SPOKE AT A MOMS' GROUP the other day. We laughed. We cried. We ate muffins together. It is good to be with other moms, talking about life and the journey we are all on. After I spoke, each table went over some sharing questions together. Our table was discussing the wildness of just getting to the group that morning. Loading up the car and actually arriving on time with kids in tow is like the parting of the Red Sea. An impossibility without an act of God. The mom next to me said, "Please tell me that it gets easier. It's not always so crazy, right?" There were some longing looks coming my way. I knew that look. I had worn it for years. The look of sleep deprivation mixed with some *I haven't been in the bathroom by myself for two years* desperation.

These were moms of preschoolers. All of their kids were five years old and younger. Those are the baptism-by-fire years. You are just trying to survive. When I had three kids aged five and under, I thought I was going down. I told the mom who asked the question, "There are different hard things about being a mom now." My kids are ten, thirteen, and fifteen. "But, yes! It gets easier! My kids can make their own breakfast now." This young mom almost started weeping with joy. The thought of her children pouring their own cereal was more than a dream come true.

I put my hand on her arm. I said, "It isn't easy right now. But you are doing good hard work." She teared up. She said, "Thank you for saying that." I got a little teary myself. I needed another muffin to get through the rest of the questions.

There is almost nothing that can prepare you for the enormity of mothering. You are so needed. There are constant bids for attention, sibling arguments, and endless chores. Teething alone is enough to break a body down. When you have young children who count on you for everything, it is easy to feel like you are going down. You feel like you will never get it all done. Here is a mom secret for you: *You will never get it all done.* It is not that you are not a fantastic mom. It is that your job is *enormous.* There is so much to accomplish and so little of you to accomplish it. Growing people up is a big deal.

Mothering is good hard work. What you are doing is so vital. So important. Nourishing young bodies, challenging young minds, shaping character, setting boundaries? These are life changers. Literally. No wonder you are collapsing in bed each night, dying for some uninterrupted sleep. You are pouring your life out every moment of every day. You deserve some chocolate and a high five.

Your good hard work is valid. God sees you each day and says, "Man, I love that girl. She is really giving it all she's got. Look how much she loves those kids." You couldn't do anything more beautiful or more powerful than nurture His own. He knows that you feel the weight of your responsibility. That you struggle with patience and that your deepest desire is to not have laundry for one day . . . Just. One. Day. He knows that you are longing for a solid night of sleep. And for wisdom . . . for all of the questions that you are asked each day. He wants you to know that He has an endless reserve of love for you that will hold you up even when you feel like you are going under. In your gigantic job of being queen, He has strength upon strength for you each day. Enough for each job that is required of you. Enough for each task that is at hand. And know beyond a shadow of a doubt that you are doing good hard work.

• • • • • • • • • • • • • • • • • •

Dear Lord, thank You for this enormous job that You have
given me, of loving and growing my child.
Please fill me with Your strength, Your patience, and Your joy.
Help me to lower my expectations of myself and place my hopes
in You and who You are. Amen.

By and large,
mothers and housewives
are the *only* workers
who do not have
regular time off.
They are the great
vacation-less class.

Anne Morrow Lindbergh

CHAPTER 4

Your Small World

I know that when I come to you,
I will come in the full measure of the blessing of Christ.

Romans 15:29

My world revolves around the lives of three boys. Their schedules. Their schoolwork. Their needs and wants. When I look at my calendar, I often wonder, *Is there anything on here that actually has to do with me? Other than going to the dentist?* And then I realize, that isn't my dentist appointment. That is their appointment, too. So much of my life is about helping them establish theirs. My care for them often eclipses my own wants and needs. And it's okay. It is why I call my mom every other week and say, "Thank you." Because I realize so much of her life was spent loving and caring for me.

Everything shifted when I had my boys. When they were younger, my life revolved around their tireless feeding schedule. Nursing, in particular, was a difficult master to serve. It is tough when your body is a dairy. Your day is chopped up into three- to four-hour chunks. You barely finish one feeding when the next needs to start. I always looked forward to introducing solid food to their diet. Freedom was just around the corner. I had a friend text me around the time that my youngest, Addison, was transitioning to solid foods. I was still nursing, but I was also feeding him baby food when the rest of us ate. She asked if we could get together for coffee. My head almost exploded. I think my incoherent text back read something like, "Sorry . . . I can't meet for coffee. . . . I am feeding this kid seven times a day!" She probably thought I had lost my mind. And I had, a little. Life was beyond full.

My days were full to the top with ordinary living. I was feeding my boys, clothing them, washing their small bodies, cleaning up after them, giving them copious bedtime kisses, and then going to bed . . . so that I could wake up and do it all over again. With babies came the reordering of my entire life. Their small world was eclipsing mine.

As your mom responsibilities grow, you may feel like your freedom is diminishing. You can't just dart off for a weekend in the wine country. Or sit down and read a single chapter of a book. Or even grab a cup of coffee with a friend, if we are being honest. Your gigantic job takes up a great deal of space in your world. The margins of your life grow smaller. It can be a tough adjustment. Some days it may feel like the walls are closing in.

But what is really happening is that you are living life to the full. To the very fullest fullness that there is. Motherhood has made your heart and your capacity to love so much big-ger. And in that widening space of your love and your care for others, there is less time to be found . . . for yourself. This is the thing. You are going to find that this mom thing has an ebb and flow to it. This season . . . whatever season of full-ness you are in, whether you are mom of an infant or a mom of teenagers . . . it is just that. A season. The small margins of your life will over time get bigger and bigger. And it is so good to recognize that along with the crazy fullness of your life as queen comes the immense fullness of blessing.

God wants to pour out His blessings on you and your very full, very good life. He will pour out His blessings even when you feel like your head is going to explode. When you are feeding people seven times a day. When you can only dream of cups of coffee and good books. Or just one tiny moment of peace. Imagine the fullness of your life, settled into the wide expanse of His caring arms. As you pour out into these little ones (or big ones), He is pouring into you. Caring for you with endless grace. Unbelievable mercy. Unstoppable goodness. Your world may feel like it has gotten smaller, but His love for you is inexhaustible. Revel in that.

* * * * * * * * * * * * * * * * *

Lord, thank You for caring for me when the margins of life seem small. Remind me of the blessings that You have for me as I face this full day. I love You. Amen.

Only God Himself
fully appreciates the *influence*
of a Christian mother
in the *molding* of character
in her *children*.

Billy Graham

CHAPTER 5

Recognizing Your Influence

Dear friends, now we are children of God,
and what we will be has not yet been made known.
But we know that when Christ appears,
we shall be like him, for we shall see him as he is.

1 John 3:2

MY SON ADDISON just got a dog for his tenth birthday. He has been begging us for a dog, he says, "for his whole life." Our whole family went to our local Humane Society, and Addie picked out a little Jack Russell terrier–Chihuahua mix and named him Flash. I told my husband, Scott, "I don't think I like small dogs." I'd had big dogs growing up. But Flash has won over my affections with his loving kisses and full-body joy. I find him adorable. He gets so excited to see us that his entire body breaks out in wiggles. I can't help responding to that joy. And for some reason, whenever I see him, I start talking like a weirdo. I don't know why. Something comes over me when I grab him up in my arms. I say, in a high-pitched squeal, "Oh my goodness! I love the puppy! He's so cute! He's so sweet. Oh my goodness!" Scott just rolls his eyes.

The funniest thing is that my weird puppy voice is catching. Addison and Will have started mimicking me. Any time that Flash gives them kisses, they start talking in the same high-pitched squeal. "I love the puppy!" and "Oh my goodness!" are shouted regularly by my two youngest sons. Scott asks me, "What have you done to them?" Nothing. I think they are talking like me because they are around me *all the time*. They hear me. They see me. They are with me constantly. They have picked up my mannerisms. My love of dance. My affinity for dark chocolate. And apparently, my weird dog-loving voice.

Moms have a huge amount of influence. Your presence is hemming in your children each day. The way that you talk, the things that you find funny, the joy that you find in the different parts of your day? Your kids absorb these things like eager young sponges. They also are shaped by your struggles, your heartaches, and your different emotions. Everything that you do is noticed. Everything that you say is filed away. Every rule that you lay down is noted (even if it doesn't feel like it). They laugh at what you laugh at. They cherish what you cherish. And they share your taste in candy, so you'd better hide it well if you want to get any of it. Whatever it is, if you like it, they most likely will like it, too (vegetables excluded).

You are an influencer. You make things happen. This is why your character is so important. Your character develops theirs. This is why your values matter and why you might want to keep cussing to a minimum. Your life is rubbing off on theirs. It makes you think twice about who is shaping you and whom you spend time with. Whatever or whoever is influencing you? They are influencing your kids.

Spending time with the One who loves you most of all doesn't just change your life: It changes your kids' lives. It is the trickle-down effect. When you are in God's presence, you become more like Him. You look and act more like Him every day. His thoughts shape your thoughts, which, in turn, shape your actions. When you talk to Him and read His Word, His mercy rubs off on you. His grace sets you free. His love encompasses you. And, in turn, your kids reap the benefits. They get in on all that goodness. They get in on His forgiveness. They get to rest in His peace. It is a win all the way around. And it just doesn't get any better than that.

. . . .

Lord, thank You for Your influence in my life.
Flood through me and pour out Your goodness on my children.
Encompass us with Your love. Amen.

A *mother* is the truest friend we have,
when trials heavy and sudden fall upon us;
when adversity takes the place of prosperity;
when friends desert us;
when trouble thickens around us,
still will she cling to us,
and endeavor by her kind precepts
and counsels to dissipate the clouds of darkness,
and cause peace to return to our hearts.

Washington Irving

CHAPTER 6

Remembering Whose You Are

See what great love the Father has lavished on us,
that we should be called children of God!
And that is what we are!
The reason the world does not know us
is that it did not know him.

1 John 3:1

THE SUMMER WHEN I was six years old, my family traveled to the East Coast for vacation. We spent a couple of days wandering the streets of Boston, walking the Freedom Trail. We stared at Paul Revere's house. We visited the Old North Church where the lantern was hung to signal how the British were coming. We threw boxes of fake tea off the side of a clipper ship like they did that fateful night of the Boston Tea Party. And we went to Faneuil Hall for lemonade. It felt like half of the world was in Boston that summer. The crowds were huge, so my mom kept reminding us, "Please hold someone's hand."

Mom didn't want any of us kids getting lost. With Jenny, Chris, and me, there was always a possibility that one of us would get distracted and wander off. Jenny was usually found by strangers and returned to us with some kind of treat in hand. I don't know how she managed this. Whenever I got lost, no one ever bought me a thing. I was usually returned to my parents red-eyed and empty-handed. I hated that feeling of realizing I was lost. It made me panicky and sick to my stomach. So I usually tried to stay close to my people. I didn't want to lose them.

Outside of Faneuil Hall there was a huge crowd gathered around a man who was eating fire and swallowing swords. It was mesmerizing. *How is he not going to burn his lips or cut his throat to ribbons?* About this time, I realized I wanted to be near my mom. I wanted her comfort if we were going to watch someone die. So I reached up and took her hairy hand. *Hairy hand? My mom's hand doesn't have hair on it!* I looked up into the eyes of giant mustached man whom I was holding hands with. He smiled at me, bemused.

I yanked my hand from his and began searching the crowd frantically. I was looking up at a whole lot of thighs and backs that I didn't recognize. Tears immediately sprang to my eyes. Within moments, my mom's hand was in mine. She had seen everything. She apologized to the man and told me, "I'm right here." The pounding of my heart subsided at the feeling of her palm against mine. I loved holding her not-hairy hand. I should have known she was close by keeping watch with her eagle eyes. I was hers. She didn't let me out of her sight.

Belonging to someone is a big deal. Knowing that you

are cared for and that someone is always looking out for you is huge. Especially if you are one of those types of people who are easily distracted and tend to get lost. The fact that someone takes great pleasure in meeting your needs gives you a sense of security. You belong to your heavenly Father. You are His daughter. He wants you to remember whose you are and who is growing you. He cares for you and every facet of your life. You can know that whatever you need, He will provide.

Knowing that you belong to God is foundational in your own mothering journey. There are so many different ways that you can struggle being queen. Every day is a new adventure. There are so many problems to solve. So many trials to overcome. Growing little people calls on all of your many talents and gifts. But one thing you don't have to struggle with is knowing whom you belong to. God cares about you and the ins and outs of your days. Just like you are watching out for your little ones, He is watching out for you. Just like you protect your kids, He is fencing you in with His protection. As His child, you can come to Him with your questions, with your hurts, and with your weaknesses. He loves everything about you. In His presence, you are always welcomed and loved. And you can rest secure in knowing that you are His. No matter what.

• • • • • • • • • • • • • • • • • • •

Lord, thank You for being my heavenly Father.
I love being Yours. I will rest secure today knowing
that You are taking care of me. Amen.

A Good Queen
Is *Not*
Jealous.

CHAPTER 7

Looking for the Awesome Sauce

*Each of you should use whatever gift you have received
to serve others, as faithful stewards
of God's grace in its various forms.*

1 Peter 4:10

My girlfriends, Jane, Tina, and Marie France, are three of the people who keep me sane in this mothering journey. For the last year, these college friends of mine and I have been texting each other each morning. We live far away from each other, but we try to stay connected because we need each other. Raising kids is no joke. Jane has a boy and a girl. Tina has two boys. And Marie France has three boys and two girls. She is the bravest of us all. Our texts are never the same. We each have different joys and struggles. We are constantly asking each other for prayer. And we all like to make each other laugh. These conversations are the highlight of my morning. The miles are bridged by our love for Jesus and our love for each other.

A few months ago, my friend Jane sent out a text about mothering that I have not been able to get out of my mind.

She said, "It's hard for me not to feel like all these other parents are better at it than me. Somehow they have figured out the awesome sauce." First of all, wouldn't it be AWESOME if there was actual "awesome sauce" to help us figure out parenting? I would buy a vat of it. And second, Jane is an amazing mom. We reminded her of that. And then we also let her know that we knew exactly how she felt. It is really hard not to compare yourself to other moms on this journey. There is always at least one mom in your circle of friends who seems to really have it all together. The keeper of the awesome sauce. How we envy her.

There are so many ways to compare ourselves to other moms and feel "less than." There are moms with all the latest gear who have the best educational toys and books for their offspring. There are the nature moms, who only feed their kids organic food and make them wear 100 percent cotton. There are the moms who are so wise, with all their patience and soft voices, who always know what to say to their kids. There are the room moms at school with their organizational skills and their ability to attend every class function. Then there are the crafty moms. The ones who make special lunches and throw theme parties and sew Halloween costumes. Unfortunately, I don't fit into any of these categories. Maybe you don't, either. But the thing that we all have to realize is that there is no awesome sauce. Each of these moms has found her own path to mothering. It is up to you to find yours.

None of us is going to mother the same way another mom does. And why is it in our nature to compare? Comparison can knock the joy right out of mothering. Just ask any non-crafty mom who has tried to make something. It makes you want to rip your hair right out. We are all different. We are all unique. Why do we think trying to be like someone else will make us a better mom?

God has created you with specific talents and giftings that fit perfectly with your own individual children. It doesn't mean that mothering your children will be easy. But it definitely won't help if you are constantly comparing yourself to other moms. Embrace the mom that you are. Know that God has you right where He wants you. He will give you what you need today to make the mothering decisions that you need to make. He has grace for you and your children. He knows you each by name and delights in how He crafted you. And that is awesome.

• • • • • • • • • • • • • • • • • •

*Lord, thank You for the individual gifts that You
have given me. Help me to become the mom
that You created me to be, and to lean into
Your wisdom as I love my child. Amen.*

There's *no way*
to be a perfect mother
and a *million ways*
to be a good one.

Jill Churchill

CHAPTER 8

Embracing Good Enough

But he said to me, "My grace is sufficient for you,
for my power is made perfect in weakness."
Therefore I will boast all the more gladly about my weaknesses,
so that Christ's power may rest on me.

2 Corinthians 12:9

I LOVE HAVING A CLEAN HOUSE. There is something so joyful about being in a home that is clutter-free. I don't love cleaning, but I love knowing that I will be able to sit down on the couch without stabbing myself with a Lego. And as a writer, for some reason I just can't be creative in a gross environment. This puts me in a bind. Because of the children, you see. Phyllis Diller once said, "Cleaning your house while your kids are still growing is like shoveling the walk before it stops snowing." So funny. So true. The dream of having a perfectly kept home flew out the window once I had kids. Everything I would do, they would undo. I almost lost my mind. I could never write because the house was never clean.

So over the years, I have learned to let go of perfection and embrace the term "good enough." I do this by keeping the kitchen clean and the front room clean. Barely. These are the two rooms in our house that we live in the most and where I write. Having two rooms in our house that are almost clean all the time gives me room to breathe, and it works for me. I can sit down and write without feeling like dirty laundry or toys are going to overtake me. How do I deal with the chaos in the rest of the house? you ask. For the children's bedrooms, I have embraced another philosophy. It's called "keep the door shut." This applies not just to the kids' bedrooms, but also to Scott's office and our bedroom on occasion. I am giving grace to myself in this area of my life. If I can't see it, it's not there. As long as the door is shut, it is dead to me. I don't have to think about it being dirty.

The philosophy of good enough has begun to shape how I see myself, too. The longer that I am a mom, the more grace I tend to have for myself. This is not because I am spiritual. It is because if I don't, I will be buried under the weight of my unmet expectations. For anyone who has ever battled with perfectionism or control issues, you get what I mean. There is something deep down inside of us mothers that longs for perfection. Not just perfection in our homes. But perfection in who we are. And the last time I checked, none of us is perfect. We want to get everything right as a mom. All the time. And it is madness. Everybody makes mistakes. Even queens. We all do things that need do overs. We can't achieve perfection. Trying to get there on our own will wear us out and make us angry.

But there is one thing that you can do. You can invite

Jesus into the mess of your life. You can ask Him to bridge the gap between the person you are and the person He created you to be. He comes in with all the wideness of His grace and meets you at your point of weakness. Jesus doesn't expect you to be perfect. He is the only One who is perfect. When He looks at you, at your heart that longs for Him and loves your children, He says, "That's good." And when you look at Him, with all His righteousness and wisdom, you can say, "You are enough." He is enough. In every situation, every circumstance, every point of weakness in your life, He is enough. He doesn't close the door on your mess. He washes you clean. He purifies you from all unrighteousness. His love covers a multitude of sins. His forgiveness sets you free. And His grace is more than enough.

. . . .

God, thank You for Your amazing grace.
You are enough for me in every situation and circumstance.
You are filling me up with Your grace even now. Amen.

A Good Queen

Always

Hopes.

CHAPTER 9

Hoping More

Be strong and take heart,
all you who hope in the LORD.
Psalm 31:24

HOPE IS A MOM KIND OF WORD. We hope new hopes for our kids every single day. We hope that they are safe, that their jeans are comfortable, that they are growing and that—*please, God*—they will have good manners when our parents visit. We hope that they have good friends and kind teachers and that they don't break any bones falling off of the monkey bars. And then we have hopes for ourselves, too. We hope that we will make the best choices for our kids, that we will grow closer to Jesus each day, and that our thighs will be smaller. Some of our hopes come true. Some of them don't. (Whatever you do . . . don't get hung up on the thigh one.) Every time we hope, there is a possibility that this hope won't be realized. Hope opens up our hearts. Sometimes our hearts get hurt. So some of us have stopped hoping altogether.

When I first started writing, I would never tell anyone when I had submitted a manuscript to a publishing company. Because it felt too vulnerable. And if I was rejected (again), I could hide it. I didn't have to share my pain and rejection with everyone. I thought that once I had been published that would change. It didn't. Wouldn't you know it, each dream, each hope, carried its own fresh new weight? Every new hope matters as much as the first one did. The disappointment is still there when a manuscript is turned down.

Last year, I was sitting in the car with my boys, getting ready to take them to school, when a call came in from my literary agent, Wendy. She let me know that a project I was hoping for wasn't going to come through the way I wanted it to. I thanked her for trying and hung up. And then I began to cry. I couldn't hold it in. My son Will piped up from the backseat, "Mom, are you okay?" I wiped my eyes and said, "Yes, I am going to be fine. I am just disappointed." And he said, "Mom, would it be okay if I prayed for you?" Then my eyes really began to water. "Yes, please, Will. I would love that." Will said, "Dear Jesus, please be with my mom. She works so hard to take care of us. Please bless her. Amen."

How is it that the dashing of one hope can open the door to the fulfillment of another? Seeing my son's heart for me was a beautiful thing. Seeing that he wanted to talk about me to the Creator of the Universe? Well, that pretty much laid me out. When our hopes reside in circumstances turning out the way that we want them to, they are fragile things, prone to leave us disappointed. But when our hopes rest in the character of the One who loves us most of all? That is a completely different story.

If our hope is in the Lord, we will be surprised again and again by His goodness and His provision. He holds us in the circle of His faithfulness. This doesn't mean that all of our hopes will be realized or that all of our dreams will come true. It means that He has more for us than we could ever imagine possible. This is the God who speaks galaxies into existence with a word. His hopes for us are way bigger than our own. His dreams for us are often impossible dreams that only He can bring to pass.

God holds your greatest hope, your children, within His grasp. He sees them and loves them more than you ever could. Whatever hopes you have for them? He has more hopes. He has created them with a plan and a purpose. He is the everlasting God with infinite resources, which He loves to use on behalf of His children. You can hope more. In His good plans. In His wise direction. And in the wideness of His all-encompassing love.

• • • • • • • • • • • • • • • • •

Lord, thank You that You hold my children
close to Your heart. Thank You that You
love them more than I ever could.
All of my hopes are in You. Amen.

My Hopes for My Child(ren)

"Mrs. Lynde says,
'*Blessed* are they
who expect nothing
for they shall not
be disappointed.'"

L. M. Montgomery

CHAPTER 10

Expecting Less

The hope of the righteous shall be gladness;
But the expectation of the wicked shall perish.
Proverbs 10:28 asv

My son Addison was walking out the door for school the other morning with a dirty shirt and a hole in his pants. We were running late. I stopped him at the door. "Where is your clean shirt?" "This is clean." "Don't you have a pair of pants without a hole in the knee?" "Nope." "I hope you at least are wearing underwear." Silence. "Addison?" "What?" "Please tell me you are wearing underwear." "I am wearing underwear." Thank God . . . a small victory won. "Are they clean?" "I don't remember." A big victory lost. I didn't ask him how long he had been wearing them. I didn't even have him go change them. Let's be honest—the children have broken me down over the years. I was just thankful he had his nether regions covered.

My mom always let us dress ourselves when we were kids. My childhood fashion sense dictated that I wear my favorite articles of clothing together. This meant that I have several photographs of me wearing a red, white, and blue halter top with pink and green flowered shorts. Favorite shirt. Favorite shorts. Boom. My mom let me do my thing. I don't know if this was because she was too exhausted to care or because she'd read in some parenting book that letting kids fend for themselves was the best way to go. But it was easy for her. Easy for me. I would be wise to follow her example.

For some reason, I had higher expectations when I became a mom. I thought that my children would wear clothes that matched, or at least that they would wear undergarments. I thought my children would look like something out of a Gap ad. In reality, their fashion sense borders more on the *Les Misérables* street urchin look. They do not care if they have holes in their pants. They don't care about wearing clean underwear . . . or any underwear, for that matter. All they expect out of life is to find some fun. They usually do. I, on the other hand, do not find the fun. Unmet expectations tend to suck the fun out of your day.

For some reason, there are quite a few of us moms who have unreachable expectations in this life. Our expectations come from a good place. Mostly because we want the best for our families. We love them. So we want good upon good upon good for them. We are not wicked just because we have high expectations. But we are probably being unrealistic. Because life is unpredictable at best. Things are not likely to go the way we think they should. High expectations have a way of letting us down. Real-life challenges can take us out at the knees. And if we are honest, our expectations can leave us disappointed.

When we have unrealistic expectations about our day or our children or even ourselves, we are basically saying, "I can't have a good day unless points X, Y, and Z happen." Everyone's X, Y, and Z are different. Mine include children wearing clean underwear. *But what if our expectations aren't met? Does that mean we can't have a good day? If life doesn't go like we think it should, is all hope really lost?* The problem with holding so tightly to our expectations is that we can't take hold of the joy that is right in front of us.

What if you were to unhook yourself from your endless mothering expectations and instead place your hopes in the One who loves you most of all? What if you decided that daily perfection wasn't your aim, but instead you opened your heart to grabbing hold of whatever joy is in front of you? It would change your outlook completely. Having a good day wouldn't hinge on points X, Y, and Z; it would hinge on the faithfulness and goodness of a loving God, no matter what this day holds for you. And if you think about it, that would actually be fun.

• • • • • • • • • • • • • • • •

Lord, help me let go of my expectations for today.
Show me how to put my hope in You
and all of Your goodness. Thank You for the joy
of this day in Your presence. Amen.

A Good Queen
Is *Not*
Proud.

CHAPTER 11

Do Overs

Because of the LORD's great love we are not consumed,
for his compassions never fail.
They are new every morning; great is your faithfulness.

Lamentations 3:22–23

THE OTHER MORNING, I put on my workout clothes to get in a little exercise with our new dog, Flash. I also put on my winter coat. Here in California, we wear snow clothes when it gets below 60 degrees outside. Flash doesn't mind the cold. He is cute and feisty. When we take our morning walk, he sniffs the whole world. He barks at fellow dogs. He tries to lunge at any cat he sees. He does his business and we head back home. It's a nice little morning routine. I feel better after being out in the early morning air.

As we were coming down the street back toward our house, I saw my neighbor. We said, "Hi!" She was getting ready to get in her car. She noticed the big jacket I was wearing. She said, "It's super cold out this morning!" I agreed and laughed. "Yes! Do you like my parka?" She laughed, too. She had one on herself. We said good-bye and I headed up the driveway to my house.

It really was so cold. *Why am I so cold?* I walked inside our house, bent over, and unleashed Flash. It was at this point that I realized that my stretchy workout pants were rolled down in the back. Like. All. The. Way. They had found a resting place under my rear. So I was basically standing there *in my underwear* framed by stretchy pants. I have some questions for my stretchy pants: *When exactly did you give out, Stretchy Pants? Why didn't I feel your downward slide? Have I lost all feeling in my lower extremities?* Mostly, I was wondering whether my parka had been covering my underwear while I was walking. *Did my neighbors have a bird's-eye view of my polka-dot panties? Did the entire world?* I felt a little nauseated. I wanted a do over. A do over with new stretchy pants, please.

As a mom, I want do overs all the time. There is rarely a day that goes by when I don't think, *Well, I could've handled that better!* or, *I am meaner than I thought.* Or, *I really need to work on that whole patience thing.* There are so many ways that the proverbial "stretchy pants" of motherhood leave us feeling exposed, vulnerable, and undone. We want to have it all together. We start out each day with our best intentions, ready to be full of love and energy. But then real life gets in the way. Kids throw tantrums or talk back. They decide to use crayons to decorate their bedroom walls. Or they lie to us about who punched whom. The craziness of life gets the best of us and we lose it.

Motherhood is humbling. It exposes you for who you really are at your core. Your temper can flare. You say something you wish you hadn't. And many days, you may end up wondering where you went wrong. And wondering how you can make it right. You need a do over. And the beautiful thing is? You get one. Tomorrow is always a do over. God's mercies never end. They are new every morning. Every. Morning. That is fantastic news, isn't it? You don't have to be the person that you are today . . . tomorrow. You don't have to behave the same way. You don't have to act the same way. You can take advantage of the new mercies that God has set aside for you. And you can ask Him to come in with His forgiveness and give you a clean heart. You can ask Him to transform you and renew your mind, shaping you into the queen of the universe that He created you to be. Daily do overs were His plan all along.

* * * * * * * * * * * * * * * *

Lord, thank You for new mercies and rich grace.
Reshape my mind and heart to look like Yours.
Show me how to love these children like You do. Amen.

Perhaps it takes
courage
to raise children.

John Steinbeck

· · · · · · · · · · · ·

CHAPTER 12

Finding Your Happy Place

You make known to me the path of life;
you will fill me with joy in your presence,
with eternal pleasures at your right hand.

Psalm 16:11

TO-DO LISTS ARE THE BANE of every mother's existence. They really are. As soon as you start writing down things that need to get done, the children start conspiring how they can keep you from getting those things done. It is lucky they are so cute. Otherwise, it would be hard to forgive them. One morning when the boys were little, I had a very specific task that I needed to complete. I had to buy our plane tickets for Christmas. My parents live in Colorado, and each year the whole family flies in to be together. Buying tickets for five people is always a chore. But with small children? It is daunting.

Jack was at school. Will and Addison were home with me, ages four and one. I was on the phone trying to use the airline's voice-automated system to purchase the tickets. Each time the voice would ask me, "What city would you like to fly to?" one of the children would yell and it would start the whole sequence over again. I told Will, "Take your brother and go in the other room." I was on the brink of a breakdown. Fifteen minutes into the call, I noticed that the children's screaming had stopped. And it was quiet. Which all mothers know is a horrible sign. Nothing good ever happens when it is quiet. I hung up without tickets and began searching for my children.

I found the boys trapped in our bedroom closet. I was unable to open the door because they had pulled every article of clothing down from the hangers and piled them up against the door. I could only open it a crack. I could see Will's eye through the slit of the door. I tried to remain calm. "Will?" "Yes." "Why in the world did you pull all the clothes off of the hangers?" "Well, I pulled a couple down . . . and then I asked Addie if I should pull the rest of them down and he said yes." "You pulled all the clothes down because your one-year-old brother told you to?" "Yes." It was in this moment that I began to think that maybe I had done something horribly wrong by having three children. Clearly, I was not cut out for this kind of work. I needed a happy place.

At some time or another, most of us moms think that our happy place is anywhere that our children are not. Maybe on a beach in Hawaii. Or tucked away in a coffee shop with a latte. Or maybe you would like to hide under a mound of clothes in your own closet so your kids can't find you. It can be hard to find joy in the middle of a messy life, when you are frazzled or stressed out. But don't give up. All is not lost. Joy can still be found. Take a deep breath and know that every day that you have with your kids will be fodder for a good memory. Especially the crazy days.

Your happy place can be found in knowing that you are exactly where you are supposed to be. Even in the chaos. Even in the madness. Even when you never get anything done. Your happy place can be knowing that God has joy for you in the mundane chores of everyday mothering and in the wild-eyed frenzy of trying to order plane tickets. That joy is found in Him. When He buoys you up with His strength. When He gives you the giggles because it might be an hour before your four-year-old can dig himself out of the closet. When He reminds you that you are doing good hard work . . . His work . . . by loving your little ones. The joy of the Lord is your strength . . . even with a never-ending to-do list.

• • • • • • • • • • • • • • • • • •

Lord, give me strength. And fill me up with Your joy as I do Your good work of loving these little ones. Amen.

My Happy Place Is . . .

_____

_____

_____

_____

_____

_____

_____

_____

_____

_____

_____

_____

_____

_____

_____

_____

_____

_____

There never was a child
so lovely
but his mother
was glad
to get him to sleep.

Ralph Waldo Emerson

CHAPTER 13

Taking Naps

He makes me to lie down in green pastures;
He leads me beside the still waters. He restores my soul;
He leads me in the paths of righteousness for His name's sake.

Psalm 23:2–3 NKJV

MY AUNT MARY SAYS THAT the first six weeks after you have a baby, you look at your bed and just long for it. She should know. She had seven babies. There is something so elemental about sleep to moms. We long for it. We need it. And yet we can never seem to get enough of it. When I had insomnia after my third baby, my doctor told me, "Imagine that every time you get a good night's rest that you are putting a deposit in your sleep bank. Every time you don't get rest, it is a withdrawal. A good night of sleep tonight doesn't make up for last night's withdrawal." I am pretty sure that thinking of all the withdrawals I had made only made my insomnia worse.

Before children, I had a heavenly sleep life. Then came the fitful sleep of pregnancy. The real mind-numbing tiredness set in during that last trimester. There were the leg cramps that would jolt me awake, the near suffocation of the pillows I had stuffed around my body to keep me comfortable, and of course, the fourteen potty breaks I had to take throughout the night. Some people said, "That is your body getting you prepared for waking up at night to feed the baby." I always disliked those people. What my body should have done was let me bank extra hours of sleep, for all the sleep I would be missing out on.

Only the fact that the children took naps saved me in those early mothering years. When they would nap, I would nap . . . or at least try to lie down for fifteen minutes and let my mind wander. I fought off the guilt of thinking I should be doing something else and flopped down on the couch. But by the time I had Addison, Jack had stopped napping. And my little windows of rest stopped with him. I survived Addie's first year in a somewhat zombie-like state.

I couldn't properly form sentences. Sometimes I forgot who Scott was. Sometimes I forgot to shower. It is a miracle we are all still alive. And now that the children all sleep through the night, I am fiercely protective of my sleep. God forbid anyone come in and wake me up before 6 a.m. I get angry inside even now. I am making up for a good nine years of interrupted sleep. When a child touches my shoulder, telling me he had a freakish nightmare, I want to say, "I don't care if you had a bad dream about eyeballs. Stay in your bed and work it out."

The thing is that more than ever, in these years of shaping little people, of being queen, you need rest. You need time to reflect and let your brain cope with all you are managing. You need moments of downtime, and you need good chunks of sleep so that your body can regenerate and heal and do all the things that bodies need to do. Just in case you feel like there is too much to be done and rest is not an option? Remember that God is good with rest. He created it. He took a rest Himself after He created the world. It is important to do your good hard work of being a mom. It is equally important to give your body and mind the space and time to replenish themselves so that you can keep doing that work.

There will always be something to clean or organize. There will always be chores to do and errands to run. You need to know that you have permission to take a nap. To rest your weary bones. To restore your mind. To know that God is enfolding you in His peace and is taking care of you—body, mind, and spirit.

* * * * * * * * * * * * * * * *

Lord, thank You for making me lie down.
Give my body the rest that it needs.
Restore my mind and spirit. Amen.

I know the well of my maternal
incompetence is deep,
but *I am determined*
to siphon up a calm
and breathing hope for him.

Donna Van Liere

CHAPTER 14

Letting Go

*Therefore there is now no condemnation for those
who are in Christ Jesus. For the law of the Spirit of life in
Christ Jesus has set you free from the law of sin and of death.*

Romans 8:1–2 NASB

IN CASE YOU DIDN'T KNOW, getting ready for church on
Sundays can be disastrous to one's mental health and spiritual well-being. For some reason, even though it is a holy day
. . . all manner of unholiness is unleashed in the mad rush
to get the children clothed and ready for church. It can be
disheartening. I believe it was on a Sunday that Will asked
Scott and me if we were getting a divorce . . . because we
were talking rather loudly (arguing) about whether or not we
should have people over without telling the other person (we
shouldn't), especially when the house looks like the "Wreck
of the Hesperus" (my mom's saying for "complete chaos").
We assured Will that we were not getting a divorce. But we
could have done with a spa day instead of a church service
after that. I'm just being honest.

I have had many, many crazy Sundays that have left me
feeling like maybe we should never go to church again. We
get an early start with the chaos in our pastor's household. I
know you are shocked. We should be more holy since church

is our job. But we aren't. And on top of not being holy, we feel really bad about not being holy. Or maybe just I do. I frequently feel the weight of condemnation. It is hard to move past the things that I have done wrong. This is something that most moms struggle with, too. Mommy guilt.

Mommy guilt comes at us from all sides. Because, for some reason, we think we should know everything there is to know about our child. We think that we should be able to meet their every need. And we think that we should be able to protect them from all pain and suffering. We also feel like we should never make any mistakes and that we should always behave appropriately (i.e., not have our kids thinking we are getting a divorce). There are a million different reasons to feel mommy guilt. Or maybe we should say that there are a million different reasons to dive into the grace that God has for us as moms.

Mommy guilt can leave you feeling completely defeated and deflated. You know that you are not going to get parenting right every time. (Sundays have repeatedly shown me that.) But living in a state of condemnation doesn't do a whole lot for your mothering skills. Is it better for you to crumple under endless thoughts of the ways that you can fail your children? Or is it better for you to recognize that you are not perfect but that you are living surrounded by God's grace and forgiveness? He has so much more for you in this journey of mothering than for you to feel like a failure. He is growing you every day. He is helping you to learn from your mistakes. He is changing your heart and shaping your thoughts. He is setting you on a path of righteousness.

Because of Him, you have freedom to grow and change and become more like Him each day. There is no condemnation in Jesus. You may condemn yourself, but Jesus is saying, "Let Me help you in the areas where you struggle. I would like to set you free." There is only one thing to do with those guilty thoughts and feelings of condemnation that are weighing you down. Let them go. Give them to the One who knows what to do with them. And feel the freedom of His grace begin to set you free.

• • • • • • • • • • • • • • • • • •

Lord, I ask You to take all my guilt.
Replace the voice of condemnation with Your truth and grace.
Forgive me for the things I have done wrong
and move me onto Your path of righteousness. Amen.

I know it is wet
and the sun is *not sunny*,
but we can have lots
of good fun
that is *funny*.

Dr. Seuss

CHAPTER 15

Soaking Up Joy

Go, eat your food with gladness
and drink your wine with a joyful heart,
for God has already approved what you do.

Ecclesiastes 9:7

WHEN ADDISON WAS IN SECOND GRADE, his teacher scheduled a field trip to Natural Bridges State Park in Santa Cruz, to witness the migration of the monarch butterfly. He really wanted me to go along. And I really wanted to hit my writing deadline. This would be a full day trip. I told him, "Addie, I am really busy. I don't think I am going to be able to go on this field trip." And he looked at me with his big blue eyes and said, "Mom? Please go. Please?" I couldn't resist his cuteness. So I signed up to drive for the field trip. I would have to squeeze in time to write later.

I had grown up near Santa Cruz, but I had never witnessed the butterflies in all of their glory. The first thing that the park rangers did before we saw the butterflies was invite us into their small museum so they could explain the monarch's life cycle. What I didn't realize was that they would use the parents on the field trip to act out the bug's life cycle. Addie's teacher volunteered me along with two dads. We were escorted to a storage closet to dress for our parts. One dad was a caterpillar. One dad was a pupa. And me? I was the butterfly. I got to dress in a black polka-dot hoodie with golden wings, black goggles, and a pair of springy feelers. We were supposed to listen for when the ranger called out our names. I was a little nervous. I knew I looked ridiculous. But then I thought, *When am I ever going to get to be a butterfly again? I should enjoy this to the full.* They called for the caterpillar, then the pupa, then the butterfly. It was go time.

I swooped into the room with my wide wings. The class was mesmerized. I did a few pirouettes. I twirled and twisted. I did a deep butterfly curtsy. Addie's teacher was dying of laughter. Addie was giggling but also looked horrified. The first-grade teacher said later that she leaned up to him and said, "That was awesome." He answered her by saying, "That was horrible." But I discovered my dance of joy. The butterfly dance. Addie might have died a little inside, but I was able to put every thought of writing and busyness out of my head. Addie and I spent the rest of the day on the beach with his class, soaking up the sun and each other. It was so good. I had figured out, at least for a moment, how to soak up the joy.

There are moments of being a mom that are so beautiful, so fun, and so joyous. And if we are not careful, we can skid right by them while we are mopping or doing laundry. We all have things that need to get done. But we will miss the beautiful part of mothering if we completely focus on the mess. These kids whom we get to hold and kiss and cuddle are pretty amazing. If we can let go of our expectations for the day and revel in the joy that presents itself, we will never regret it. You will find yourself exhilarated. And so will your child.

God created you with joy in mind. He is blessed when you enjoy the life and the children He has given you. He is thrilled when you explode with laughter, when you clap with happiness, when you cry with tears of laughter. He is all about joy. If there is a moment when you can share joy with your kids—do it. If you can find time every day to make your child laugh or horrify them with your terrible dancing—do it. If you can squeeze in a moment of play when you remember one more time what it feels like to be so little and so alive—do it. Enjoy your life. It is a beautiful, wild thing.

*Lord, thank You for the joy that being a mom brings me.
I love to laugh and play and be with this little one.
Remind me one more time that joy
has been Your plan all along. Amen.*

A Good Queen

Is

Patient.

CHAPTER 16

Inviting God into Your Day

Taste and see that the LORD is good;
blessed is the one who takes refuge in him.

Psalm 34:8

MY OLDEST SON, JACK, is now a teenager. One of the things that I have noticed about him over the past few years is that he is growing quieter. With me. As a little boy, Jack was a fountain of information. He could not wait to tell me about what had gone on at school that day. He always had a story to tell about class or what happened at recess or whom he had played with that day. He would pepper me with facts about the things that he was learning. The conversation would start the minute that he got in the car, and it wouldn't end until we got home. And then came the onset of teen-hood.

It's not that Jack has withdrawn. He still likes to talk. But the things that matter most to him he keeps to himself. The things that trouble him take a long time to surface. And drawing him out is like a game of twenty questions. The other night we sat on the couch and I said, "Jack, when I was your age, I liked so many boys." Silence. "I really did.

I thought they were cute. I liked a different one every couple of months." "That's great, Mom." "So . . . do you like any girls at school?" Silence. "Any of them that you think are cute or nice?" More silence. "Jack, you can tell me." Jack turned and looked me in the eye. "Mom, go to bed." I just started laughing. I get it. I would have rather died than have told my mom or dad who I liked when I was Jack's age. But the thing is, I do so want to be a part of Jack's life. I want in on all of the nitty-gritty details. I want to help him sort through life and figure it out. It's what moms do. I just love him so much. I am willing to wait for the moment when he invites me into his life . . . however long it takes.

The crazy thing is that we take after our heavenly Father in this way. He wants to be a part of our day because He loves us so much. He is interested in the nitty-gritty details of our lives. He would like to help us sort out the ins and outs of our days, if we will let Him. But unlike me, He doesn't force His way into the conversation. He wants us to engage with Him. He is waiting for us to invite Him into our day. This can be as easy as starting a conversation with Him when you wake up. When you are in that space between awake and sleep, you can shoot up prayers to the heavens, calling on the One who loves you most of all.

I call these early morning prayers "ceiling prayers." They are simple. And to the point. *Help me, Lord. Be with me. Show me how to love You and the people You have put into my life. Thank You for this beautiful day.* If you are sleep-deprived, "Help" works just fine. You can let Him know what you think that the day is going to hold for you and ask that He would guide you, give you wisdom, and—please, Lord—an extra helping of energy and strength. The thing is that God wants in on your life. He loves you so much.

In Psalms it says that God delights in the details of our lives. And He has endless resources to meet your needs. He has a deep well of love that He draws from, and He would like to pour it out on you. He wants to guide you down paths of righteousness. You can start out your day by taking refuge in His goodness. And who knows what He will do with your day when you invite Him in? The possibilities are limitless.

. . . .

Lord, I am inviting You into every corner of my day.
Lead me, guide me, and know that
I want to share my hopes and dreams with You. Amen.

My Ceiling Prayers

A Good Queen
Is *Not*
Irritable.

· · · · · · · · · · · ·

CHAPTER 17

Counting on the Crazy

In their hearts humans plan their course,
but the LORD establishes their steps.

Proverbs 16:9

THE MOM LIFE IS completely unpredictable. Some days are crazier than others. The dishwasher explodes. The car battery dies right before you have to take the kids to school. One of the children has a nervous breakdown in the middle of the grocery store. These aren't anomalies. Things like this happen regularly to me as a mom. I wish I could say it was different once the children got older. Somehow things just never turn out that way.

My son Will is a daredevil. It's not that he wants to injure himself. It is just that the thought, *Well, that looks like fun,* goes through his head quite regularly. And then ten seconds later we have an injury. We know the ER well. I had a glass cloche that I used to use as a decoration on our coffee table. Will came into my room one morning wearing it on his head. I told him, "Will, that is super dangerous. If that broke, you could cut yourself very badly. Please do not play with that." He complied. Two minutes later the crazy broke loose. Will limped into the kitchen weeping with a huge cut on his back. Instead of wearing the cloche like a hat, he'd tried to sit in it. This did not go well. It was on a Sunday morning, of course, because things are always crazier on Sundays. So we were off to the ER for stitches. Again.

As a mom, it might be a good idea for you to just count on the crazy. "Count on the crazy" is the mom version of "expect the unexpected." You are a mom of little people whose main goal is to enjoy life every moment of every day. Their enjoyment will not necessarily segue into your enjoyment. The crazy will happen. But it is your choice if you let the crazy completely derail you and make you lose your mind. You can decide whether you want to fall apart or whether you want to take a deep breath and say, "Here is the crazy."

What if each time something crazy happened, like a tantrum in the supermarket or the dishwasher leaking on the floor, you thought, *Yep. I was counting on this.* Not in a fatalistic way. But in a way that helps you to say, "Here is the crazy . . . I am okay. We will survive this. And this can still be a good day." Wouldn't it take some pressure off?

What if instead of starting off your morning with an expectation of nothing ever going wrong, you started off your morning with the prayer, "God, I have no idea what is going to happen today. I have some plans I have made, but I want You to establish my steps. I want You to mark out my path. I am placing all of my hopes for today, all of my dreams, all of my wishes, in You. I am going to follow Your lead, even when it is crazy." You might actually be able to breathe.

God knows that being a mom can be wild. Almost every day. But He still has good things for you in spite of the craziness. Your well-being and expectations can't be rooted in the hope that your day turns out the way you want it to. Your well-being needs to be anchored in the hope that God will be with you in the ins and outs of our days. Through the unspeakable joys of mothering or the crazy chaos. Your soul can be moored in the fact that God is who He says He is and He will do what He promised, working all things together for the good of those who love Him. That includes dead car batteries and ER visits. As you trust Him with your crazy, He will establish your steps. He will order your life. And He will wrap you in His arms of peace and hold you close.

. . . .

Lord, I know it might be crazy today.
I want You to establish my steps today.
I am trusting You in all things. Amen.

Courage!

*(Said with a fist raised in the air
and a French accent)*

Jennifer Foth Moody

CHAPTER 18

Being Encouraged

Therefore encourage one another
and build each other up, just as in fact you are doing.
1 Thessalonians 5:11

SIX WEEKS AFTER having my third baby, Addison, I found myself in the parking lot of Target. I had all three boys in the car with me. Jack was five. Will was two. Scott was at work. And I was going to the store for the first time as a mother of three. I sat for a good ten minutes in the car. It felt so good to know that everyone was strapped in and safe. I called my sister, Jenny. "Hello?" "Jenny, I am in the parking lot of Target with all three boys . . . and I am scared to go in." Grocery shopping with tiny children is a task for the fearless. "Sue, you can do this. I believe in you! You know what they say in Senegal?" For years my sister worked overseas in Africa at a nonprofit, and she speaks French. "The French say, 'Courage!' It means to take heart. Have courage." I said it back to her: "Courage!" I unbelted myself. "Okay, Jenny, I'm going in!" Sometimes motherhood is like a military mission . . .

get in and get out as fast as you can. You need your sisters-in-arms to cheer you on and bolster you up.

I found early on in mothering that I couldn't hang out with people who were negative. I needed encouragement and solidarity in my friendships. I didn't have a lot of extra energy for difficult relationships. My relationships with three tiny boys were all the difficulty I could cope with. I was doing all I could to feed three little kids and still love my husband. Those were my parameters. When friends wanted more of me than I could give, I had to be able to say, "This is me. It's not pretty. I almost always will be a wreck. If that works for you, I would love to hang out. Oh, and I need you to be okay with me canceling on you on a moment's notice due to stomach flu. If you are good with that, I would love to be friends. And I'll do the same for you in return. You have my back, and I will have yours."

Good friendships and encouragement are necessities for moms. Like air and chocolate. It seems that other species know this innately. I was reading up on whales for one of my son's school projects. A pod of whales is more than a group of giant creatures swimming together. They are a community that takes care of each other. They seek out food together. They protect each other from predators. The mom whales band together to raise the baby whales. If one mom can't feed her baby, then another whale steps up. Pods are beautiful things. On more than one occasion, I have had a friend feed my kids, step in with hugs, or watch them for me while I was trying to hit a writing deadline. These people are my mom pod. We pray for each other. We lament together. We cheer each other on. We are soldiers in the same battle.

God gives you dear mommy friends during different seasons of mothering. You can teach each other, lean on each other, and shout out, "Courage!" when some daunting mothering task has you pinned down. He has designed you for relationship. He has given you your mom friends, the ones whom you can be honest with, whom you can cry with, and whom you can share your deepest fears with, to build you up. These are your pod. Your community of encouragers. You can give each other hope on dark days and laugh together when life as a mom seems impossible. And you can celebrate like crazy when the good stuff comes along. And being a mom of sweet little ones or fun big ones? There is more good stuff than you can imagine.

* * * * * * * * * * * * * * * * *

Lord, thank You for my friends.
Help us to build each other up
and to cheer each other on. Amen.

I would maintain that *thanks* are the highest form of thought, and that *gratitude* is happiness doubled by wonder.

G. K. Chesterton

CHAPTER 19

Being Grateful

Give thanks in all circumstances;
for this is God's will for you in Christ Jesus.

1 Thessalonians 5:18

COMPLAINING IS ONE OF THE WORST sounds in a mom's ears. It is a fingernail-on-the-chalkboard kind of sound after you have spent the day serving your kids. Doing laundry. Washing dishes. Making meals. You have poured yourself out in a wide variety of tasks to ensure your children's health and safety. Then to have someone say something like "I don't like chicken tacos" after you have spent an hour making chicken tacos? It can tend to grate on one's nerves. The words that most moms would love to hear scattered throughout their day are "thank you" or "Mom . . . you're the best!" or "Wow . . . you really are doing an unbelievable job of shaping my life and character." (That last one is highly unlikely, but it would be nice.) My son Jack came up to me in the kitchen the other day and said, "Thanks for lunch, Mom." It changed my entire mood. I could have kissed his face all over. But then he would never say those words again.

Words of gratefulness are like balm to the mommy soul. Your good hard work has been recognized and appreciated. When the children are grateful for all that you do, it is wonderful. On the occasions when the words of thanksgiving fall unbidden from the children's lips and are accompanied by a hug and kiss? It's as if the heavens have opened up and rained down joy. Gratefulness is that good.

The crazy thing is that while I am constantly reminding my boys to be grateful, I regularly forget to be grateful myself. Almost every day. Recently I have had one of those convicting Holy Spirit thoughts poke my brain. The kind of thought that says, *There is so much that I do for you on a daily basis. But when you talk to Me, you just tell Me all the things you don't like about your life.* I realize that I complain to Him a lot more than I thank Him. I rarely enter His gates with thanksgiving. I enter them more with a whine of *Why hasn't this happened the way that I want it to?* And I often enter His courts with "not-so-much praise." I unload all of my problems at His holy feet without a single thank-You for the endless blessings that He pours over me. I had a much worse problem of ungratefulness than my kids do.

Sometimes, when you are a mom, your child is like a tiny mirror, showing you your own heart, your own weaknesses. I have so much to be grateful for. Life. Love. Grace. Mercy. Hope. Forgiveness. A loving husband. Three beautiful boys. A close-knit family. Good friends. A home. Food on the table. The career that I longed for. Health in my body and mind. Everything. There is so much more in my life to be grateful for than there is to complain about. Gratitude should be the way that I start and end my day.

When you decide to be grateful, it changes your mind-set

about life. When you recognize all that God has done for you and is doing on a daily basis, it gives you a much-needed gratitude adjustment. You are who you are and where you are today because of Him. It is good to unleash some thanks to the heavens. Pepper your day with some cheers and hip-hip-hoorays. God is continuing a daily work of drawing you to Him. He has gone out of His way over and over again to bless you. He has bent over backward to comfort you in times of sorrow and hold you close when you are afraid. He has given you joy upon joy in this life with your little ones.

God is deserving of all of your praise, your thanks, your wonder, and your marvel at His great works in this world and in your own life. He loves blessing you. He loves giving you good gifts. And He responds to your thankful heart with His sustaining faithfulness and His all-encompassing peace. Once you get started thanking Him? It is easy to get carried away. So go for it.

• • • • • • • • • • • • • • • •

Lord, thank You. Thank You. Thank You.
Thank You for who You are and all that You have done for me.
I am overwhelmed by Your goodness. Amen.

I Am Grateful For . . .

A Good Queen

Is

Kind.

CHAPTER 20

Healing Words

The tongue has the power of life and death,
and those who love it will eat its fruit.

Proverbs 18:21

WILL GOT IN THE CAR the other day and told me, "Mom, you look pretty and you smell nice." I almost passed out from the singular joy of that moment. Most of the time my boys say things like, "Hey, Mom . . . did you know that there is a lot of gray in the front of your hair?" Or "Mom, I can't look at you when you dance . . . it is embarrassing." Whenever one of them says something kind or complimentary to me, I am overwhelmed. It fills me up. Kind words, especially from those whom you love so much, are life-giving. Will saying that I looked pretty was more than a compliment. It touched my soul.

Those of you who have mothered for any length of time may have realized that words hold a lot of weight. How you speak to your family members, how you address your children, how you correct and discipline them, can set the tone for your whole day. Your emotions and tone can make the difference between you feeling filled up or deflated. Your words hold power. Your kids' words hold power. And you can choose to use them for good or use them for evil.

When I used to teach preschool, we would always encourage the children to use their words, not their hands, to express how they were feeling. We would say things like, "Tell him how you are feeling instead of hitting him." Or, "Can you use your words and tell us why you are crying?" It doesn't take long, though, to realize that words can also be used as weapons. They can cut and bruise the spirit of both you and your child. I always try to remember that before I have had coffee in the morning and I am teetering on the brink of exhaustion. It is easy to say things I don't mean if I am not in a good place emotionally or if I am sleep-deprived.

School mornings seem to unleash the verbal beast within me. It is the stress of trying to get somewhere on time that launches me into attack mode. "Why didn't you make your lunch last night like I asked you to?" and "You are making everyone late. Go brush your teeth now." Somehow my ability to use my words, my kind words, fails when we are heading out the door. So I decided that, like a preschooler, I needed a reminder to use my kind words.

I have a chalkboard in my kitchen where I write down prayer requests and Scripture verses. I wrote out the verse, in giant letters, "You shall go out with joy and be led forth with peace," as a visual reminder so that I remember to bring the joy and peace each morning with my words. As I am getting my coffee, that joyful beverage that sets the world to rights, I remember that I make a difference when I choose my words carefully. I can send the kids out into their day with my nagging reminders, or I can choose to speak light and life over them.

God speaks light and life over you every day. His Word encourages you and lifts you up. His discipline is always backed up by forgiveness, love, and grace. He sets the tone for your day with how He speaks to you. He doesn't need coffee to use kind words; it is just in Him. When you speak with kindness and grace to your little ones, you are not only setting the tone for their day, you are buoying their small spirits. You are building them up and sending them out with peace and goodness. Just like your heavenly Father does for you.

* * * * * * * * * * * * * * * * * *

Lord, unleash goodness and kindness from my mouth today.
Remind me that my words hold the power
of life and death. Thank You for speaking life
over me with Your Word. Amen.

My mother's menu
consisted of
two choices:
Take it or leave it.

Buddy Hackett

CHAPTER 21

Nurturing Small Bodies

For he has satisfied the thirsty soul,
and the hungry soul He has filled with what is good.
Psalm 107:9 NASB

WHEN I WAS IN KINDERGARTEN and first grade, I went to an elementary school about six blocks away from my house. At lunchtime every day, my two older sisters and I would walk home from school for a hot lunch that my mom made for us. My brother, Chris, wasn't in school yet. When we would get home, the four of us would crowd around the kitchen table for lunch. During the winter, I remember steaming mugs of hot chocolate waiting for us along with our grilled cheese sandwiches. If we were cold, Mom would tuck blankets around our little legs to warm us up before the walk back to school. I didn't mind the extra walk home, even when it was cold. Having those moments with Mom were special. That break in the day from schoolwork wrapped us in her love and her nurturing care. Maybe that is why we ran the last block to the house. We couldn't wait to get there.

Not only is my mom a fantastic cook, but she is a fantastic

nurturer. There were always special things that she did for us that let us know we were loved. My dad was a pastor of a growing church. There wasn't a lot of money for extras. But she always made sure that we had a new pair of good shoes for school, with lots of room in the toes for growth. And we girls always had a new dress for Easter and a new dress for Christmas. Chris would get new outfits to match, which I am sure he loved. To me, this was a huge deal. Being the youngest of three girls, almost all of my clothes were hand-me-downs. One year, Mom made us matching Holly Hobby dresses with poufy bonnets. We looked like Mary, Laura, and Carrie from *Little House on the Prairie.* No girls have ever been more proud of their bonnets.

Somehow Mom knew the secret desires of our hearts. When I was in first grade, there was a Halloween parade. The only costume to be found was Jenny's old clown costume. I wanted to be a fairy princess. It is hard to be a fairy princess in a polka-dot jumpsuit. I don't know how Mom did it, but she found time to sew me a pink tutu. It was the most beautiful thing I had ever seen. The tulle was crisp, and there were pink sequins on the shoulder straps. Of course, I had to wear a turtleneck under it and a winter jacket over the top of it for the outdoor parade. October in Illinois can be biting cold. But I was so proud of the pink frilly fluff peeking out of the bottom of my jacket. I remember Mom standing along the parade route on the playground and grinning back at me as I waved my wand at her.

Food and clothes . . . such basic life essentials. But Mom

made them more than that. They were the physical embodiment of her love for us. We felt sheltered in her care. There was always something warm to wear and something good to eat on the table. With each meal, each item of clothing, Mom was ministering to us in the most basic of ways. Telling us we were loved. Special. Worth taking care of. Because of her attention and love, we weren't just growing taller, our souls were being nurtured.

God does the same for you. Taking care of your most essential needs. Providing you with everything that you need every day. He loves you so much. He always wants to show you His loving care. And as you care for your children, you are mirroring His goodness and faithfulness. Each meal on the table flows from His abundance and assures your kids that they are special and worth taking care of. Each pile of clean laundry speaks volumes about how you are clothing these little ones in your love. You are hemming them in with your kindness. You are surrounding them with your goodness, showing them their worth. Just like your heavenly Father does for you.

• • • • • • • • • • • • • • • •

God, thank You for Your provision and care.
I see Your love for me in the details of my life.
Help me to show Your care to my children. Amen.

A Good Queen
Is *Not*
Rude.

CHAPTER 22

Cleaning Little People

*Do not merely look out for your own personal interests,
but also for the interests of others.*

Philippians 2:4 NASB

BEING A MOM IS NOT for the faint of heart . . . or for the faint of nose. In case you didn't know, you are not only the queen of the universe, but the queen of a stink factory. There are a whole lot of smells that accompany young children . . . and older children. You are constantly wiping down your children. It seems their job is to make messes and yours is to clean them up. Smelling their necks to make sure that no milk dribbles have snuck down into the creases. Changing diapers. Bathing small bodies. Washing tiny hands. Lotioning, powdering, baby-wiping. The mess is not contained to their bodies. You are also cleaning yourself up. Because somehow their dirt seems to make its way onto your clothes, as well. Spit-up on your shoulder. Sticky handprints on your thighs. The cleanup never stops.

You must subject yourselves to a wide variety of uncleanliness in the growing of little people. When my youngest,

Addison, was learning how to feed himself, he decided to use his food as a hair gel. By the end of each meal, his fine hair would be fortified with some type of vegetable or fruit, or if he was lucky, with syrup. He would sit there in all of his food glory with a tiny Don King hairdo. This type of hairstyling always required more than a baby wipe. It needed the full force of the kitchen sink or remnants of breakfast could still be seen at dinner.

These days, with puberty lurking around every corner, I am not just keeping my children clean for my own pleasure. I am doing it for the world at large. I don't want to hurt their feelings. I am not trying to be rude. I just want them to have friends. I want them to understand that the odors that their bodies are emitting can keep them from forming close bonds with the rest of humanity. Brushing their teeth isn't just to promote strong enamel . . . it can also promote strong friendships. Summer vacation does not mean that you can take a vacation from showering. Now before my children go out to the car each morning, I ask the questions, "Did you brush your teeth?" and "Do you have on deodorant?" Sometimes they lie. They say, "Yes." But my nose tells me differently. Then I have to become more invasive in my tactics. "Let me smell your breath." And, "Let me smell your armpits." This is never pleasant for either of us. The boys are offended by the invasion of their privacy. I am offended by the smells attacking my olfactory senses.

I have also been known to say things randomly like, "Why am I smelling feet?" and "Why is your hair a grease slick?" Again, I am not trying to be rude. It's just that these are important questions to ask. The offender is sent off to the shower amid great protest. It is also important to be very clear about what a "shower" actually entails. I say, "Use a lot of shampoo on your hair. And make sure that every inch of your body is covered in soap . . . *every inch*." Otherwise, the child will take a three-second shower, lightly spritzing his entire body with mist, without actually cleaning any part of it. I know that they will thank me later. But the world is thanking me now.

God has given you a monumental task in trying to keep your children clean. He knows this. But He also knows the beauty of caring for someone down to the minutest detail. He does this for you every day. He cares for every inch of you. Your mind. Your body and your spirit. It is not a glamorous task. But it matters. He has given you the physical care of your children. Caring for every inch of them. Keeping them clean is such a small part of what He has tasked you with. But it matters. And in all honesty, there is nothing more delightful than holding a snuggly little person, fresh from the bath, wrapped in a towel. Or hugging a giant teenager whose armpits have been freshly deodorized. You are shaping the world with lavender soap and minty toothpaste. Showing your children how to care for their bodies and, in turn, care for those around them is good clean work. You are loving them in the details.

• • • • • • • • • • • • • • • • • • • •

Lord, thank You for placing these children in my care.
Show me how to love them in the details.
Wrap us up in Your love. Amen.

A Good Queen
Endures
Through Every
Circumstance.

CHAPTER 23

Controlling Yourself

But the fruit of the Spirit is love, joy, peace, patience,
kindness, goodness, faithfulness, gentleness, self-control;
against such things there is no law.
Galatians 5:22–23 NASB

POTTY TRAINING CAN TRY THE SOUL of the heartiest of mothers. I always hoped it would magically happen on its own. It did not. My sister Jenny says she will never forget the day when I walked into the living room and saw something I never wanted to see on my white slipcovered chair. I looked at my youngest child and uttered the fateful words, "Did that come from your mouth or from your bottom?" Jenny started gagging right then and there. But it was an important question . . . Was I dealing with the stomach flu or a lapse in potty training? Neither was a great option. But at least the stomach flu was usually just a twenty-four-hour bug.

I learned early on that motivating a tiny person to try to use the bathroom is tricky. There has to be a great reward involved to lure them away from the ease of diapers. I mounted a sticker chart on the bathroom wall. A new sticker was placed on the wall each time there was a successful trip to the potty. And when the small boy was finally accident-free, a big prize was brought forth. A visual testament to the hard work that was accomplished. Learning to control your body, on any level, is a huge accomplishment.

Potty training is just the first step in teaching our children how to control their bodies. But the mind-set is helpful as the children get bigger and the stakes get higher. There are so many different ways that we have to learn to control ourselves . . . and teach our kids to do the same. It can be hard to do, but the reward is there if we commit to it. It's the committing part that is so difficult. It is so much easier to take the easy way out and not discipline ourselves. We need self-control when it comes to eating, good sleeping habits, screen time, knuckling down to do homework, managing money, and organizing our living space. We get to model self-control to our kids. But sometimes our "modeling" isn't the best. Our areas of weakness can bleed over into their lives. I would much rather eat chocolate and watch TV than munch an apple and pay my bills. My kids would join me in my lethargy. I'm just being honest. But that is where the Holy Spirit comes in. His life in us. His will at work in us. When we invite Him into our lives, we get all of the benefits of who He is, working out His plan in our lives and hearts.

God wants the best for you and He brings out the best in you. He is encouraging you to have self-control just as you are encouraging your kids. Leaning into Him, you sense His direction. His leading. His delight. Making good choices, being disciplined, having self-control yields big rewards. It brings peace and health and joy along with it. Maybe you need a giant sticker chart on the wall to remind you that when you practice self-control and allow the Holy Spirit to do His good work in you, you reap the benefits. And not only do you reap the benefits, but so do your kids. They get to see what life looks like with the Holy Spirit at the helm. They get to see the joy that comes from letting God take the lead, helping you make good decisions for your life and your body. And that is a beautiful thing.

• • • • • • • • • • • • • • • • • • •

God, thank You for the work of Your Holy Spirit in my life.
Thank You for the work of Your Holy Spirit in my children.
Lead us in the way that we should go. Amen.

A Good Queen
Is *Not*
Boastful.

CHAPTER 24

Having Manners

I will give You thanks with all my heart;
I will sing Your praise before the heavenly beings.
I will bow down toward Your holy temple
and give thanks to Your name for Your
constant love and truth. You have exalted
Your name and Your promise above everything else.
Psalm 138:1–2 HCSB

THERE IS NOTHING I LOVE MORE than giving gifts or little treats to Scott and my boys. I love the way that their eyes light up and the joy that creases their faces. Gift-giving is my love language. I always try to give my kids something that will delight their hearts. It doesn't have to be big. It just has to connect with something that they love. Jack loves books. Will loves paper to draw on. Addie likes little toys to play with. I love bringing happiness into their day.

My oldest son, Jack, is the same way. He starts planning out his brothers' Christmas gifts in early November, socking away loose change and searching online for good deals. He researches video games. He hounds his brothers with questions. And then, once he gets their presents, he can't wait to give them to them. He can't wait to see their excitement. So, on Christmas Eve, he hides their presents and gives them a sheet of paper with clues. It is a Yuletide scavenger hunt. There are shouts of joy and laughter as Will and Addison race through the house, trying to find the little treasures that Jack has hidden for them. The only thing that deflates Jack's joy is if his brothers forget to show their appreciation. Which happens. Because they sometimes forget about Jack while they are enjoying the toy at hand.

This is where I step in. "Will and Addison . . . is there something that you would like to say to your older brother?" "Thanks, Jack." "Thanks for what?" "Thanks for the present." "And?" "What?" "What else did he do for you?" "Oh! Thanks for the scavenger hunt." "Give him a hug." At this, Jack balks. "That's okay, Mom." He is grinning. I am training the boys in the art of manners. Sometimes manners have to be dragged out of them. But that's okay. This is important stuff that will help them throughout their entire lives.

The wheels of this world are greased with "Please" and "Thank you," as far as I am concerned. When I am reminding my boys to say "Please" and "Thank you," it isn't just so they can be polite. It is a way for them to acknowledge all that they have been given. When I tell the boys to say "Please," they are releasing themselves from a sense of entitlement. That they can take what they want, when they want it. It is important for them to remember that everything that they need comes from someone else's hand. And when I remind the boys to say "Thank you," it encourages a thankful heart for the gifts that they have been given. So much of what we receive in this life comes from the generosity of others.

"Please" and "Thank you" work for moms, too. These are the two most powerful prayers that you can pray. What gifts haven't you been given by the One who brings you joy? When you say "please," it releases you from a sense of entitlement. You get to recognize that God is the Giver of good gifts. It has nothing to do with your own merit—it has everything to do with His generosity. You can brag about who He is and what He has done for you. He will give you everything that you need in just the right time. He delights in giving to you, and He is delighted when you respond with praise. When you say "Thank You," you are recognizing the bounty of His blessings. He pours out His grace and mercy on you daily. He gives you food and shelter and love. Every day you are surrounded by the abundance of His household. "Please" and "Thank You" are foundational words in your daily conversation with the One who loves you most of all. They are good words to hear and even better words to say.

• • • • • • • • • • • • • • • •

God, You are so good to me.
Thank You for all You have given to me.
You are the ultimate Gift-Giver. Amen.

I am sure that if the *mothers*
of various nations could meet,
there would be *no more* wars.

E. M. Forster

· · · · · · · · · · · · ·

CHAPTER 25

Learning Kindness

Be kind and compassionate to one another,
forgiving each other, just as in Christ God forgave you.

Ephesians 4:32

I DON'T KNOW WHY it is so difficult to be kind to your siblings.
I remember it being very hard as a child. Somehow I felt like
they always had it better than me. So I took out my aggression on them. With some meanness. Some hitting. The occa-
sional elbow to the gut. I am not proud of it. I am just telling
you how it was. The last thing on my mind was treating
my sisters and brother with kindness. The realization that I
actually liked my siblings came with age. And because my
parents *made* me be kind. They wouldn't tolerate the meanness. But I seemed to pass on the "mean" gene to my boys.

The unkindness in our family all began when Will was
born. Jack did not take kindly to his younger brother. He felt
like Will was invading his space. The first time we went to the
park together, when Will was six weeks old, Jack leaned over
in his car seat and bit Will's teeny-tiny toe. He drew blood.
There was some deep-rooted aggression there. When Addison
was born, Will responded differently. He tried to love Addie
to death. He would lie full-out on top of his baby brother,
smothering him with kisses. Addie had a desperate look in his

eye. He needed intervention and some oxygen. Of the three boys, Addison is the toughest. Probably because he has been fighting for his life since infancy.

I have taken up the cause of kindness. Just like my parents, I am *making* my boys be nice to each other. It is the "fake it until you make it" approach. I make them apologize to each other when they are mean. I give them consequences when they punch each other in the neck. I remind them that someday they will view each other as their greatest allies, but for now, they at least have to pretend to be nice. Sometimes pretending is all I can get from them.

Loving the ones we live with can be difficult. Siblings seem to get on our last nerve. But there are breakthrough moments. There are shining pinpoints of kindness that give me a glimmer of hope. The other day, Addison bought a pack of gum when he went to the store with me. Gum is a special treat in our house. We don't get it all the time. But when we got home, the first thing Addison did was offer a piece to each of his brothers. Without any bribery, coercing, or pressure on my part. I just kept quiet and watched the beauty of kindness unfold in my own home. I didn't want to jinx it. And then I watched both Jack and Will take a piece of gum and say, "Thanks, Addie." Without me saying, "And what do you say to your brother for being so nice?" They said "thanks" because they actually wanted to. Because they were being nice. I just had to sit back and soak it in.

Loving-kindness is so attractive. It is what draws you to the heart of your heavenly Father. You are drawn to His mercy and grace. You are drawn to His generous spirit and His wide ocean of forgiveness. You are drawn to the immense wealth of peace that you sense in His presence. And in those moments, when you let that kindness, that grace, that mercy, that peace show through, it draws others to you. Kindness knits your hearts with the ones you care about. It strengthens your love for each other. It helps you all to extend grace to each other even when you don't always get it right. When you are kind, when your children are kind, you look a whole lot like Jesus. And that is beautiful.

· · · · · · · · · · · · · · · · · ·

Lord, help me to show kindness to my children.
Fill their hearts with Your kindness, too.
Let us look more and more like You every day. Amen.

My mother was the most beautiful
woman I ever saw.
All I am I owe to my mother.
I attribute all my success in life
to the moral, intellectual,
and physical education
I received from her.

George Washington

CHAPTER 26

Teaching Little People

Let my teaching fall like rain
and my words descend like dew,
like showers on new grass,
like abundant rain on tender plants.

Deuteronomy 32:2

THE FIRST DAY THAT JACK went to kindergarten was like a door cracking open on a new life for me. Now, instead of having three children aged five and under to take care of, I would only have a three-year-old and an infant at home. There was a great sense of freedom beckoning me. So I did what every young mother does when their firstborn goes to kindergarten. I stood in the school courtyard and bawled like a baby. My friend Melissa cried with me. Her daughter, Grace, was also starting kindergarten. The school administrator, who was a friend of ours, walked past us and said, "Come on. Give me a break." He had seen kindergarten moms break down for years. He knew our kids would be fine. We moms were another story.

As a mom, you are your child's first teacher. I taught Jack all I knew to teach him before school. About manners. About going to the bathroom on his own. About listening carefully. About eating healthy. Every moment of every day for the last five years, I knew what he was up to. And now there would be huge chunks of his day that I was going to know nothing about. Watching him line up for his first day of school was the first moment I truly realized, *Someday Jack is going to grow up and he is going to leave.* This was the first set of wings I was giving Jack. He was taking a leap without me. The administrator was lucky that I didn't lie down on the concrete and weep.

Every day that I was with Jack, I was learning from him. And now, when he was at school, I was going to miss out on a great deal of his humor, his hugs, and his logic. He taught me that if one sock falls into the toilet, to be sure to throw the other sock in so that it wouldn't be lonely. He taught me that more than anything, we want our family members to go to heaven . . . even if that means you should tell your two-year-old brother he is going straight to hell if he doesn't ask Jesus into his heart. And he taught me that you should try things . . . even if you are scared . . . because it might be fun. I was learning so much more about life by being with Jack. I was realizing in that mere moment, my time with Will and Addie would shift, too. It goes by so fast . . . this teaching, learning time.

All of my boys are in school now. Our time together is shorter, but I am still learning from them. I see them face new situations head-on. They each approach life differently. Addison attacks it. Will embraces it. Jack reasons with it. They all have unique things that they have revealed to me about myself. They have taught me to be more patient. They have taught me to look for fun. And they have taught me about love. Unconditional, unbridled mom love. I am fiercely proud of each of them. In a small way, I want them always to be near me. But mostly, I want to see them soar. To grab hold of this life and live it to the full. These boys have taught me what the father heart of God is like.

God wants you to soar. He has taught you how to live life to the full. He wants you to embrace this path that you are on, the mom path, the teaching path, and soak it up. This good hard work that He has given you to do only lasts for a season. Then these little birds are going to head off to kindergarten and someday to a life of their own. (Try not to collapse on the ground thinking of this.) And you are going to know that you have had a small, beautiful part of grounding them in love and giving them wings. There is no better work than that.

* * * * * * * * * * * * * * * * *

God, thank You for teaching me through my child.
Give him wings to soar
and a heart to follow after You. Amen.

My Children Have Taught Me . . .

Some are *kissing* mothers
and some are *scolding* mothers,
but it is *love* just the same,
and most mothers kiss
and scold *together*.

Pearl S. Buck

CHAPTER 27

Saying and Doing

*Trust in the LORD with all your heart and lean not
on your own understanding; in all your ways submit
to him, and he will make your paths straight.*

Proverbs 3:5–6

MY MIDDLE SON, WILL, reminded me yesterday that I owe him a dollar. "Mom, you owe me and Addie money." "I do? What for?" Let's be clear. I wasn't doubting that I owed him money. My brain has a way of forgetting things these days. I just didn't remember what the money was for. "Remember, you said that you would give me and Addie a dollar if we could sing all the words to the song we were dancing to?" "Oh yes!" I do occasionally pay the children to sing and dance. It is highly entertaining. And a lot cheaper than paying to go see a musical. "Go look in my purse." He was happy. I was, too. I actually followed through on something.

One of the great plights of motherhood is follow-through. There are so many commands and directives throughout the day. So many questions asked and so many answers to be given. So many consequences and rewards to mete out. It is hard to keep track of them all. Especially when it comes to discipline, you can get lost in a haze of blind threats and empty promises. "If you don't clean your room, you won't get to play with your toys." Or, "Do what I asked you to do or I will add an extra chore to your list." Or, "Please use a kind tone with me or I will be talking to your father." The follow-through is the hard part. You actually have to do what you say you are going to do.

I never realized when I was a child that follow-through was important. I always hoped that my parents would forget whatever wrongdoing I had done and not give me any punishment at all. I also didn't realize that it is hard to follow through with promises as a parent. Whether it is a treat you promise to give your children or a time-out for talking back, it can be exhausting work. There is a constant barrage of questions and demands that your sweet little ones make. There is no such thing as a day off for the queen. You need to be able to take time and think about how you want to respond to each question and situation. And if you don't follow through right away, you really do forget what you have told your kids you would do. That can begin to erode your child's trust in your word.

I have come up with a workable solution. I have stopped promising as much. Or laying down edicts. Or giving out impossible punishments. Because I want my word to mean something and I want to be able to follow through. I want my kids to trust what I say. I use these phrases quite a bit: "Let me think about it," and "We'll have to wait and see," and "I need to talk to Dad about that." I want to have a plan that I can stick to. I want my kids to see that I mean what I say and I say what I mean, and that usually takes some forethought and planning. And I always want to keep my promises so that my kids can find me trustworthy.

God is the best at keeping promises. He is completely trustworthy. He always says what He means. He always follows through. He keeps His promises. And His promises are phenomenal. If you trust Him, He will make your paths straight. He will establish your plans. He will help you to flourish. He will protect you. He will be with you. No matter what. When you walk in His path, when you keep your promises, when you do what you say you are going to do, you become trustworthy, just like He is. And that is a great thing to be.

• •

Lord, thank You for Your promises.
Help me to follow in Your path
and be trustworthy like You are. Amen.

Journey mercies.
Watch your
blind spots.

Sandy Schroeder

CHAPTER 28

Showing and Telling

*Start children off on the way they should go,
and even when they are old they will not turn from it.*

Proverbs 22:6

LEARNING HOW TO RIDE A BIKE is one of the greatest accomplishments of childhood. My husband, Scott, is a pro at teaching bike-riding skills. He taught all three of our boys how to ride their bikes, how to find their balance, and how to fly down the street, yelling with joy. Freedom on two wheels. I tried to help Addison learn to ride his bike. Once. Not because I didn't want to help him anymore, but because I almost killed both of us the one time I tried. I got Addie firmly seated on his bike, helmet on. I grabbed the back of his seat and said, "Okay, Addie, you start pedaling and I will run behind you!" He gave me the thumbs-up and started pedaling like there was no tomorrow.

There is a science to teaching someone how to ride a bike. You have to keep the same pace and judge the right time to let go, so that the new rider gets a healthy push in the right direction. I took off running, clutching the back of Addie's seat to steady him. We began to pick up speed. Addie was getting the hang of it, keeping the bike balanced. Halfway down the block, I caught my toe on a raised edge of the sidewalk and pitched headfirst into a clump of juniper bushes. Of course, I forgot to let go of the bike. So I basically pulled Addie down on top of me. We were both stunned. One minute he was flying . . . the next he was using me as a human airbag. "Are you okay?" Addie got up and brushed himself off. "Yeah, Mom, I'm okay." He surveyed me in the bushes. "But let's have Dad help me ride from now on." I said, "Good call." I lay there for a while. I needed some time to gather myself.

There are quite a few similarities in training kids to ride a bike and training them how to live out life. You are excited and kind of scared, not knowing whether you are getting it quite right. You want to aid them as much as possible but let them learn how to make a go of it on their own. There are moments when all goes perfectly. And then there are the moments when you face-plant into the shrubbery and take your child down with you. I'm just saying. Showing them how to live life is hard. But once you show them the ropes, once they see the goodness of life when you are following the One who loves them most of all? They will never forget it. All the life lessons that you share with them? All of the commands that keep us hemmed in by God's goodness and love? These become ingrained in them.

Whenever we leave on any type of trip, my mother-in-law, Sandy, always tells us, "Journey mercies!" and "Watch your blind spots!" She always wants us to stay safe. These encouragements go a long way in the mothering journey. We need God's mercy every step of the way. And we need Him to watch out for us in the areas where we are blind. The mom journey is fraught with pitfalls and, apparently, really pokey bushes.

We are showing our kids the way to go, how to travel God's path, and how to live. Even when you don't realize it, you are showing your kids the way of hope. You are walking out (or face-planting in) life as a Christ-follower. When you mess up, you are showing them how to pick themselves up and get life going in the right direction again. You are giving them a healthy push in the right direction.

As you seek God and who He is, you are bringing these sweet kids along on the journey. They are seeing His faithfulness. They are tasting His goodness. They are grasping the whys and hows of living a life in the care of the Creator and that is a good thing. And it is something that they will never forget. Even if they get sidetracked. God's truth has a way of nestling in their hearts and lingering in their souls. The truths of who He is have shaped their minds. He calls to your kids as they grow and leave your home, and He reminds them that their truest, best life is found in Him.

• • • • • • • • • • • • • • • • • •

God, as I show my children how to follow You,
impress Your goodness upon their hearts
and shape their minds with Your truth. Amen.

Always remember
that you are unique.
Just like *everyone else*.

Margaret Mead

CHAPTER 29

Realizing What You Have

I praise you because I am fearfully and wonderfully made;
your works are wonderful, I know that full well.

Psalm 139:14

WE HAVE A SUMMER TRADITION of having a garage sale as soon as school gets out. The boys love it. They go through their toys and books and video games looking for the items they are willing to part with. And we usually have a lemonade stand to aid in sales. This is where Jack found his true calling. Salesmanship. From the very first garage sale he participated in at the age of six, he was a fearless beverage hawker. It was in him. He had no fear. He scoffed at rejection. As soon as someone would arrive, he would begin his pitch. "Lemonade! Twenty-five cents! Free refills! Lemonade! Twenty-five cents! Free refills!" This he would continue the entire time the person was browsing, sometimes walking behind them as they were looking around. And while I was proud of his tenacity, a few times I reeled him in with, "Jack, they heard you, love," or, "Okay, Jack, that's good." I didn't want the person to feel uncomfortable being trailed by an overeager kindergartner.

But over time, I have thought a lot about Jack and his tenacity. I have thought about how we view life as children. When we are brand-new to this world, testing the waters, we are fearless, and mostly we think that people love us and accept us. We are comfortable in our own skin, and we like who we are. And as I watched Jack with his skills, hawking lemonade like a used car salesman, I realized that this was Jack in all his fullness. Not toned down or pulled back or chided because I was uncomfortable with his outgoingness.

The truth is that Jack is a masterpiece. Created by the Creator of the Universe to be like no other human ever created. Completely himself. Completely made in the image of God. Completely lovely . . . as is. So is Will, with his wild, unabated energy. And Addison, with his fierceness and drive to make people laugh.

I have decided, as a mom, I don't want to be the one who tones Jack down and covers him up. I don't want to be the one who shapes Will into a mini-me with my same tastes and talents. I don't want to be the one who battens down the hatches on Addison's courage. I would like to be the one who lets Jack be the Jack, and Will be the Will, and Addison be the Addison that God created them to be.

Sometimes in the shaping and growing of little people, we moms can get overzealous in wanting our kids to be exactly who we think they should be. We can forget that we have been given the gift of a completely unique, one-of-a-kind individual to shape and mold and kiss as much as we can. Who will not be exactly like us. Or their dad. Or their uncle Bob. There is something so beautiful about the realization that there never has been and never will be another child quite like yours. Her personality, her laugh, her hairline, her quirkiness. His boldness, his big eyes, his thought process, his talents. When we realize their unique beauty, we can stand back and revel in it . . . not try to change it.

God has made you to be completely unique, too. Your thoughts, your smile, your talents, your joys. All your very own. And He loves how He made you different from everyone else. He would like you to love how He made you, too. He sees you, in all of your beauty, and He doesn't want to tone you down in the least. He wants you to shine. To be all that He has created you to be. And to bring glory to Him as only His child could. He treasures you. You are a one-of-a-kind masterpiece.

* * * * * * * * * * * * * * *

Lord, thank You for my child's uniqueness.
You have created my child as a masterpiece of Your love.
Show me how to help her shine. Amen.

My Child Is a Masterpiece Because . . .

What greater *aspiration*
or challenge is there
for a mother than the *hope*
of raising a great
son or daughter?

Rose Fitzgerald Kennedy

CHAPTER 30

Keeping Focused

*Brothers and sisters, I do not consider myself
yet to have taken hold of it. But one thing I do:
Forgetting what is behind and straining toward what is ahead,
I press on toward the goal to win the prize for which
God has called me heavenward in Christ Jesus.*

Philippians 3:13–14

WHEN ADDISON WAS THREE, he was invited to a birthday party of one of his little preschool buddies who was turning four. The party was taking place in a karate dojo with some basic instruction from a sensei, who would show the kids how to kick and block and tumble across the mat. Addison was painfully shy. Just a year earlier, he would have burst into tears if someone made direct eye contact with him. We were still working things out in group settings. So when the kids were invited out onto the mat, Addie wouldn't go. My friend Katie, whose son was having the birthday, said to me, "Sue, just come out with him. I will go out, too." She didn't want Addie to miss out on the fun.

So there we were. Me. Addison. Katie. And twelve four-year-olds. Blocking. Punching. Yelling, "Kee-yaw!" I was enjoying myself. Addie? Not so much. He was mostly standing by my side. He wanted to sit down and watch the other kids.

He wasn't thrilled with me yelling and punching the air. He really wasn't thrilled when it came to the kicks. And it was at that point that I "Kee-yawed" and kicked Addie instead of the air. It's not pretty when you take your three-year-old out with a bloody lip. The birthday fun was over. Addie and I hightailed it out of the dojo and went to the burrito shop next door for some ice for his fat lip. And I bribed him with a Coke. Because that is what you do after you injure your child. I held him close and told him I was sorry and that I wouldn't ever do high kicks again. He forgave me. It was harder for me to forgive myself.

There have been several mothering instances when I have wronged my boys. Things I have said to my boys. Times when I punished the wrong child, only to find out who the guilty culprit was later. Or those moments when they were longing for my attention and I brushed them off to do laundry or chat with a friend on the phone. I only noticed the hurt look in their eyes after it was too late. These are the "mommy fails" that we wish never happened. Just the other day, Addison prayed, "Dear Jesus, please help my mom not write any more books." It was an eye-opener. Clearly there needs to be a re-arranging of priorities when your child starts praying against your career. I am still learning. Hopefully, I am a better, wiser mom today than I was yesterday. Learning and changing is part of the journey.

It is easy to feel like you are failing regularly as a mom. There are so many things to get right that can go wrong. But you are in this for the long haul. Your mommy fail today can be a jumping-off place for reflection. There is a call for you to be gentle with yourself instead of beating yourself up. You can keep moving forward instead of mulling over yesterday's mistakes. Or high kicks, for that matter. Every day, Jesus is transforming you into His image. Every day, He is shaping your heart and changing your thoughts. Forgetting what is behind, leaning into His grace, propelled by His truth, you get to keep pressing toward the prize. And the One who loves us most of all? He is cheering us on.

* * * * * * * * * * * * * * * * * *

Lord, I am keeping my eye on the prize today.
Keep changing me and leading me. Bless these little ones
and surround us with Your grace. Amen.

A *mother* is one
to whom you hurry
when you are *troubled*.

Emily Dickinson

CHAPTER 31

Being Together

For where two or three gather in my name,
there am I with them.

Matthew 18:20

SUMMER HEATWAVES ARE MY UNDOING. Living near San Francisco Bay, our home doesn't have air-conditioning. The ocean breeze off of the water is supposed to be enough to cool us down in the evenings. Except when it isn't. When it is over 90 degrees inside your house, your butter melts into a puddle on your kitchen counter. The children become cranky and forlorn. And you start to consider resting your forehead on the toilet lid, just for some cool relief. During a heatwave, it usually feels hotter inside of our house than outside. This might be because when I am hot, my children gather around me and want to lie on me. I try to explain to them, "Mommy is so hot. And maybe a little angry. When you put your hot skin on my hot skin, I feel like I might explode into flames." The children don't understand this. They think, *I feel horrible. If I lie on my mom, I will feel better*. Welcome to motherhood. You will never be alone again. Even when you are hot.

Being together is something that moms are designed for. Even in the wild, mama animals are followed relentlessly by their young. You can understand why the mama birds push the little ones out of the nest. Maybe all the extra feathers are making them hot. They need some alone time. Even though the closeness of the ones you love so much can be difficult at times, this season of togetherness is not all bad. In fact, it is beautiful. Being together can nourish your soul. Tiny kisses on your face. Leg hugs. Small bodies snuggling close to yours as you read to them. All of these experiences are so precious. Because junior high is not that far off. You will find, in the blink of an eye, that your wish to be alone has come true. All of a sudden the children will not want to be with you. The children will want some alone time. Snuggling? Out of the question.

We were designed for "together." Alone is good and necessary. But together is better. Your kids need you close for your guidance, your wisdom, and your warmth (or your volcanic body heat). They need the reassurance that you are there for them no matter what. And you need their beautiful smiles, their words of affirmation, their butterfly kisses, and their side hugs (junior high). You are more of who you are supposed to be in each other's presence. You are walking out the journey that God has set in front of you when you pull your child close and hold them. You are affirming who they are and their worth with your love, with your time, with your affection, and simply by being you.

The amazing thing is that when you are together with your children, God is right in the middle of the mix. He loves you all. He loves how you are working out life together. He is on hand to guide you and give you great heaping amounts of patience and goodwill when you don't have an air conditioner. He is with you when you can't seem to get a moment's peace. And He is reminding you that this "togetherness" that you are doing all the time? It is His idea. He is moving in you and through you. Growing you and your children into the people you were designed to be. Together.

• • • • • • • • • • • • • • • • • •

God, thank You that I get to be with my children.
Help me take full advantage of our togetherness.
Remind us daily of Your nearness. Amen.

Keep looking up.

Opal Blakeley

CHAPTER 32

Laughing More

A cheerful heart is good medicine,
but a crushed spirit dries up the bones.

Proverbs 17:22

A WISE PERSON ONCE SAID, "If Mama ain't happy, ain't nobody happy." More than almost anything . . . I love to laugh. Finding something silly or funny to throw back my head and belly-laugh about is the best. But I won't lie. There have been some dark mothering days for me. It's not all roses and sunshine. Life is hard. Money can be tight. The kids can be cranky. And I am not always happy. I have struggled off and on with depression since having my third son. It has been a journey of learning myself. Of figuring out how to take care of myself so I can take care of these kids whom I love so much. And it has been a journey of finding a new path to joy.

There was one very pivotal session in which my counselor said very gently, "I think you are dealing with some unrealistic expectations." Then she said, "Let's figure out some ways to help you find some joy in your day." Those words set me free. Because we all need some joy in our day, don't we? Joy in your day. Pep in your step. A light in your eyes. A giggle on your lips. These are things that we all long for. But sometimes life works against us and leaves us hurting.

Usually when we are feeling overwhelmed, we also feel alone. We pull away to nurse our wounds. But the thing is, healing is usually a two-person job. We need others in our lives to point us in the right direction. To encourage us. To put an arm around our shoulders. And to let us know that we are not alone.

My sisters and my cousins, Beth and Gretchen, were my go-to people during my time of learning how to navigate life with joy. They were safe. They knew me. They loved me. They cried with me. And we could laugh, sometimes right in the middle of crying. How is that possible? I think because God has a way of cracking open the door to joy when we are in pain. He gives us glimpses of truth and hope that free up our souls, if we let Him. With all the weightiness of my depression, I needed to know that the world still held some light and some laughter for me.

They lit up the dark with their presence. Their laughter lifted me. It wasn't that they didn't recognize the darkness that I was going through; it was that they were stepping into it with me, encouraging me to keep moving forward. To take it one day at a time. Reminding me that this was a season of the soul and it wouldn't always be that way. I love them for that.

My grandma Blakely always used to say, "Keep looking up." In those dark moments of life, when we are not sure what is coming our way, we can know that God has joy for us. Laughter heals us from the inside out. Joy has a way of bringing our chins up when we feel beaten down by life.

God's plan is always to build us up, heal us, hold us close, and bring us closer to Him and His love with each step. Joy is His idea. It is a byproduct of life with Him. Even in the midst of pain.

If you have a chance to laugh, take it. If your kids do something funny, savor it and tell as many people you can about it. Joy builds upon joy. If there is a moment for joy in your day, grab it with both hands and know that you are surrounded by the light and love of the One who loves you most of all.

• • • • • • • • • • • • • • • • • •

Lord, show me the joy that this day holds.
Remind me of Your love and light.
Thank You for bringing me closer to You. Amen.

My mother had a slender,
small body, but a large heart—
a heart so large that
everybody's joys
found welcome in it,
and hospitable accommodation.

Mark Twain

CHAPTER 33

Celebrating

And on that day they offered great sacrifices,
rejoicing because God had given them great joy.
The women and children also rejoiced.
The sound of rejoicing in Jerusalem
could be heard far away.

Nehemiah 12:43

SOME DREAMS ARE A LONG TIME in coming. When I first began writing, I never knew it would take me ten years to get my first book published. I was sitting in the grocery store parking lot when the call came through from my agent that I was being offered a book contract. I started crying and laughing at the same time. Dreams can be like that. Scott and I had our three boys in the car with us. It was an ordinary evening. We had just pulled in to grab some milk. And then my life changed forever. It was almost bedtime for Jack, Will, and Addison. But instead of driving home, we drove to our favorite outdoor café with the fountain and live music. And we ordered chocolate cake and hot chocolates all around. Even for the eighteen-month-old. Because some celebrations are worth double chocolate. If there is something worth celebrating, do it right.

My mom was the chief celebrator in our home. It didn't have to be a huge occasion. It didn't have to be a birthday or a special holiday. Sometimes it was as simple as recognizing that a fear had been overcome or someone had gotten an A on a test. There was always an ice cream cone promised on the first and last day of school. Sometimes we used three cheers to celebrate: *Hip! Hip! Hooray!* And there were always plenty of hugs and kisses to go around. I remember, in particular, one afternoon when my mom made her first batch of olallieberry jam. It was a triumph. My mom, who is usually a very calm and rational woman, linked arms with us kids and began dancing around the kitchen, saying, "Mommy makes good jam! Mommy makes good jam!" It was true. She really did. We celebrated with a dance. We celebrated with hot buttered toast with generous dollops of delicious jam. We celebrated with great joy! Life was good and beautiful and sweet, and Mom was showing us the way.

Life is full of exhilarating highs and sometimes unexpected lows. In case you haven't figured it out yet, life can be hard. I know that is a truth that none of us wants to hear. But there is another truth that counterbalances it. God is doing good things on our behalf . . . all the time. Every day. There are moments every day when we can shout for joy, give some thanks, and eat a piece of toast with delicious jam. When we celebrate the life that we have been given, we are honoring the One who gave it to us. When we celebrate with our kids, we are showing them how to do the same thing. We are reinforcing the thought and the value that life is precious. It is a gift to be enjoyed and savored. When we open our hearts to joy in the small things, we train ourselves to be open to joy all the time.

Don't be afraid to go all-out. Do a dance in the kitchen. Grab a candy bar and have an impromptu snack in the backyard to celebrate the first day of sunshine after a cold winter. Clink cups of water and say, "Cheers!" when the house is clean and you can all collapse on the couch for a snuggle. When good things happen, don't let them slip by unnoticed. You were made for these moments. Your little ones were, too. God loves celebrations. He is planning on throwing a huge party when we see Him face-to-face. We are just getting in a little practice here on earth.

• • • • • • • • • • • • • • • • • •

Lord, show me what to celebrate today.
Open my heart to the things You are doing in my life.
Thank You for the beautiful life
that You have given me. Amen.

10 Reasons to Celebrate

1. _____

_____

2. _____

_____

3. _____

_____

4. _____

_____

5. _____

_____

6. _____

_____

7. _____

_____

8. _____

_____

9. _____

_____

10. _____

_____

My Favorite Songs to Sing with My Child

1. _____
2. _____
3. _____
4. _____
5. _____
6. _____
7. _____
8. _____
9. _____
10. _____
11. _____
12. _____
13. _____
14. _____
15. _____
16. _____
17. _____
18. _____
19. _____
20. _____

I'll take you *once*
every day of the week
and *twice* on Sunday.

Alice Croisdale

CHAPTER 34

Singing Lullabies

The LORD your GOD is with you,
the Mighty Warrior who saves.
He will take great delight in you;
in his love he will no longer rebuke you,
but will rejoice over you with singing.

Zephaniah 3:17

I USED TO ROCK ALL OF MY BOYS to sleep when they were little. I loved the feeling of them in my arms. The weight of their little heads on my shoulder. As I would rock, I would sing to them. I could feel them relax and melt into me as I sang "Jesus Loves Me" and "Jesus Loves the Little Children." Then I would sing worship songs. It was a mini worship service in the rocking chair. They would fall asleep, and I would hold them even though I could have put them in their beds. Mostly because they were so cute and I loved the smell of their little necks and the feel of their wispy hair resting under my chin. Oh, how I loved those babies. As Scott's Granny Alice used to say, "I would take them once every day of the week and twice on Sunday."

Now my boys are getting big. And soon I am going to be the one who can sit on their laps. And I miss some of those moments when they were little and they would come to me longing to be held. I still get a few hugs and kisses. But the other night, as I was tucking Addie into bed, he said, "Mom, can you lie down next to me?" It was an invitation I couldn't refuse. I lay down on the bed and stretched out next to him. His feet are almost as big as mine now. And then he turned on the pillow and said, "Mom, will you sing to me?"

With my forehead next to his, I sang him the songs of his babyhood. The *Veggie Tales* songs that he loved. The worship songs that I used to sing when I rocked him. And he closed his eyes and just listened. And then he said, "Sing another one, Mom." I kept singing. And we were there cocooned in the joy of being together.

A few months ago, my middle son, Will, stood next to me in church. Worship had just begun, and it was a good loud song. I could hear Will next to me. He was actually saying the words. We raised our voices together, singing out about the God who had created us. I don't know what Will was thinking about as he was singing. But I know what I was thinking. That I loved hearing his strong, clear voice. I loved feeling him stand next to me shoulder to shoulder. I loved that the words of truth in the song were pouring over him, filling him up. I loved that he was with me and in the presence of the One who loved him most of all.

Singing is a powerful thing. Whether you are rocking your babies, snuggling next to them, or standing in a church pew, the truth that you sing out changes you and the ones you sing with. When you sing with your children, you are echoing the words of the heavenly Father over you. You are mimicking His delight and His joy in His children. You don't have to have a good voice. You just have to have a good, strong mommy heart to do it. A heart filled with love that pours out over those sweet big and little children whom He has given you. And know that as you are singing your heart out, God is rejoicing over you both. He delights in you. He is beside Himself with joy each time you show your kids His love. Each time you spend time caring for them. Buoying them up with words of truth. Reminding them that they are hemmed in on every side by the love of the Father. That is something to sing hallelujah about.

* * * * * * * * * * * * * * * *

Lord, thank You for who You are.
Let my voice always be raised in praise to You.
Let Your song and Your truth surround my children. Amen.

A Good Queen
Never
Loses Faith.

CHAPTER 35

Minding Life

And the peace of God, which transcends all understanding,
will guard your hearts and your minds in Christ Jesus.

Philippians 4:7

THE OTHER DAY, I was lying down on the couch, trying to take a ten-minute rest before I had to pick up the boys from school. Life is full. You have to squeeze in little bits of revitalization where you can. My phone rang. I didn't recognize the number. It was my son Will. "Hi, Mom." "Hi, Will. What's going on?" "Are you coming to get me?" "Yes." "When?" "When school gets out." "Mom . . . school is out. It's early pickup today." "Then I am coming right now." I heard a sigh on the other end of the phone. "Okay, Mom." The children have to put up with a lot of disappointment. My mind is not what it once was. I used to think I was a pretty intelligent woman, but things can start slipping during motherhood. "Mommy brain" is a real thing. The struggle is not imaginary. And sometimes I feel like I am losing the battle.

When Addison was three, I once took him in to the on-call doctor because I suspected that he had croup. The barking cough. The fever. It all added up. The doctor asked me, "Has he ever had croup before?" I looked at him. I looked at Addie. I said, "Well, I know one of them has had croup."

153

"One of them?" I laughed. "I have three boys. Sometimes I get them mixed up." He laughed and said, "Ahhhh . . . it all makes sense now." "What does?" "We doctors have a saying about moms...with the birth of each child, you lose about a quarter of your brain." I didn't even laugh. It seemed like a realistic equation to me. After three births, I am now surviving on a quarter of the brainpower I once had. I feel the lack every day. Being queen can do that to you.

Being a mom requires so much of your thought processes. Every day, not only are you taking care of yourself, but you are also taking care of another or several other little people. You must remember everything about them. If they are tiny, you actually have to remember to feed them. Regularly. So they can stay alive. You have to keep watch over them every moment and protect them from all harm. You have to keep relearning them with each new stage of development and remember to make sure that you have enough diapers or clean underwear. There are so many things to manage and so many things to remember.

The amount of information that you have to retain for each child is astronomical. You are overloaded with information. Your mommy brain isn't small. The truth is that your responsibilities are expansive. There are so many details about these little ones whom you love so much that have to be quantified and dealt with. Toss in a little sleep deprivation and it is no wonder that you can't recall the last time that you had the oil changed in your minivan. Or which children in your child's class have peanut allergies. Or whether or not you have actually showered today. Don't lose heart. Take a deep breath and relax.

God has created you with a magnificent mind. And the mind of a mother is a wonder to behold. You are fearfully and wonderfully made. You are formed with a fantastic capacity to take care of other human beings. Every day, your brain cells are taking care of business. Sometimes you may forget a few things. But have faith in yourself and have faith in the God who orders your universe. You are doing huge work every single day. You are feeding, clothing, encouraging, loving, and building up a young person. Grounding them in the wide peace of God and the truth that they are worthy and loved. That same peace surrounds you as you navigate motherhood. Lean into that peace. Remind yourself of it. The God of all of creation is renewing your mind, strengthening your spirit, and holding you close every day.

• • • • • • • • • • • • • • • •

Lord, thank You for the magnificent mind
that You have given me. Keep renewing my thoughts
and lifting me up. I love knowing
that I am surrounded by Your peace. Amen.

Everybody wants
to *save the Earth*;
nobody wants
to help Mom
do the dishes.

P. J. O'Rourke

CHAPTER 36

Laboring with Love

*No one should seek their own good,
but the good of others.*

1 Corinthians 10:24

I HAD JUST RETURNED HOME from a trip and was greeted by a familiar sight. A ginormous pile of laundry. The way that my children generate dirty clothes, you would think they get paid for it. They take their dirty-clothes work very seriously. As I loaded up the washer and added extra fabric softener, one of the children said, "Yay! The Laundry Fairy is back!" Another one piped up, "And the fairy who fills up the water jug in the fridge is back, too!"

It's nice to think that some mythological creature is doing all of the grunt work in our house. What I wouldn't give some days for a whole legion of fairies to swoop in and vacuum, mop, de-stinkify, bleach, scrub, and wipe down my house. The Mount Everest of towels in my laundry area has been known to cripple me on sight. But in our house the Laundry Fairy, the Dinner Fairy, the Wash the Windows Fairy? All me. Okay . . . I'll be honest. I rarely wash the windows. Only when the handprints get so bad that we can't see through the glass do I whip out the window cleaner. But still . . . the chores? They never end.

I am a firm believer that since the children are contributing members to the mess of the house, they should also be contributing members to the cleanup of the house. Our boys have daily and weekly chores. I am teaching them how to cook and how to separate the lights from the darks in the wash. They tend to balk at any new chore that I try to teach them. When I tried to show my youngest, Addison, how to do the laundry, he looked at me and said, "But I am just a baby." He was nine at the time. I told him, "It's time to be a big boy." Teaching them how to work hard can be hard work in and of itself. The truth is that being a mom requires a whole lot of hard work. Even when you are teaching the children how to do the housework . . . you are still doing housework. Sometimes you might just want to give up and embrace the filth. I won't lie. I know I have given it some serious thought.

The thing is that all labor is a labor of love. All that you do for and with your children shows your true heart for them. All those chores? All those dishes that arrive piping hot and sanitized? And dirty T-shirts that come out of the dryer fresh and clean only to be dirtied again? All the vacuuming and dusting and folding of clothes and filling of water jugs? You aren't necessarily doing these things because you like to . . . you are doing these things because you love your kids. You are meeting their needs with good food. You are growing their bodies and hearts and minds with your loving care. You are showing them what real love looks like: servanthood. Putting their needs before your own. Offering them a life of security and clean linoleum.

The dailiness of your work shows the constancy of your love. All you are doing for them is for their good. For their benefit. When you load your dishwasher, you can think, *One more load of love for my family.* And when you are folding all those tiny pairs of shorts and bleaching barf stains out of bibs, you can say, "Look at all this good clean love going on here." You are pouring out your life for your family with love, with goodness, and sometimes, even with joy. And that is all good.

* * * * * * * * * * * * * * * * * *

Lord, thank You for modeling servanthood for me.
Show me how to love my family
with the daily-ness of my work.
Surround us with Your overwhelming love. Amen.

Life is more *fun*
if you *play* games.

Roald Dahl

CHAPTER 37

Playing Hard

God saw all that he had made, and it was very good.
And there was evening,
and there was morning—the sixth day.

Genesis 1:31

YESTERDAY I TOOK MY BOYS to their grandma and grandpa's condo. Scott's parents live in a neat community tucked up against the San Francisco Bay. The best thing about the condo is the fact that we get to go swimming in the pool every summer. My oldest son, Jack, wasn't sure that he wanted to swim. Because he is a teenager. But I let him know that everyone would be swimming. Because it is summer and it is hot and pools, even borrowed ones, are a gift from God. Within minutes they were all chasing each other and laughing. I lay on a lounge chair and chatted with my mother-in-law and told the children not to kill each other. There was to be no jumping on your brother's head, pulling at his neck, or hanging on his ankles. People could die. But have fun. These are the things that I say when they swim with each other.

I know the lure of the pool. I spent many hot summer childhood days in pools, making whirlpools and playing mermaid. There were hours upon hours lost in play and imaginary seascapes. Chicken fights were won and lost.

Breath-holding techniques were perfected. But the absolute best moment came when my mom or dad would come in the pool, too. They would break the parent/kid barrier. They would paddle next to us. Dad would launch us into the air like waterlogged missiles. Missiles of joy, that is. As soon as we would land with a splash, we would go back for more. We also liked to use my mom as an air-flotation device. All four of us kids wanted to hang on her and be near her. We loved seeing her laugh. She always tried to do laps, and we never let her. Because we wanted her to play.

Yesterday, the most frequently asked question was, "Mom, when are you coming in?" My boys aren't little anymore. But they still want me to play with them. Jack and Will want to race me and show off their freestyle skills. They can beat me now with their long muscles and broad strokes. And Addison wants to hang on me . . . like an air-flotation device. If he can, he wraps both arms around my neck and trails me in the water like a giant boy cape. And we laugh. Almost the whole time that we are in the water. I have entered their world of no bills and sunshine. It is glorious. Until someone dunks someone else, and then I am the enforcer again, meting out punishments. But for a few moments, we are eye to eye, bobbing in the water, soaking up the wonder of God's creation laced with chlorine.

In our mom-ness, we can forget the delight that the world holds for us. Because of all the work. But the best part of our good, hard, world-shaping work is when we are eye to eye with the ones whom we love, laughing and caught up in joy. There are moments every day when your kids will call you out to play. And you should. Because the dishes are never going to get done anyway. And laughing is better than being angry. Your kids are wonder machines, engaging with the world around them. You get the rare privilege of entering that space when you play. God must love having fun. Because all of His creation wants in on joy. He thinks joy is good. He thinks His creation is good. He wants you to enjoy the world He made. He wants you to enjoy the little people that He has given you and get caught up in the wonder of the world around you. What's stopping you?

Lord, I love that You have created me and my kids for joy.
Show me the ways that I can engage with my children.
Thank You for the wonder and delight
that You have brought to today. Amen.

There are only
two lasting bequests
we can *hope*
to give our children.
One of these is *roots*;
the other, *wings*.

Johann Wolfgang von Goethe

CHAPTER 38

Holding On

But solid food is for the mature, who by constant use have
trained themselves to distinguish good from evil.

Hebrews 5:14

My aunt Mary raised seven boys. I lived with her and my uncle Terry for a year before I got married, and five of the boys were still at home. The thing that amazed me most was how calm Aunt Mary seemed. She just took things in stride and laughed a lot. I asked her how she did it. How she could raise so many boys? Wasn't it hard to see them leave? I was on the cusp of starting my own life with Scott. I wanted all the wisdom she could give me. She held out her cupped hand and closed it. She told me, "I have always thought of my boys like butterflies. When they were so small I kept them very close." Her hand began to open gradually. "I taught them everything I could. The older they get, the more freedom and responsibility I give them." Her palm flattened out. "And if I have done my job right, when they are ready to leave home, they will be ready to fly." Holding on. Letting go. That is the plan of motherhood.

I picture that opening hand every day when I am with my own boys. Am I teaching them everything I can? Am I giving them more freedom and more responsibility? Because, really, there are moments in this wild world when I want to clamp my hands shut and keep these butterflies at home . . . until they are thirty. That is the opposite of holding on and letting go. Holding on and letting go means giving your children a solid foundation to leap from when they are ready to launch out on their own. Giving them boundaries and letting them test the limits. Showing them the way and then watching them make mistakes. Helping them learn to walk but letting them fall down. They need to be able to master life on their own. It is hard not to be a "smother" mother. Fixing everything. Making it right. Keeping them safe. But I know if I keep them too safe? If I don't let them make mistakes or fail or get hurt living in the real world? I will never give them the wings they need to fly. It's a crazy balancing act of holding on, tethering them to the truth of God's love, and encouraging them to leap into the life they were created for.

When Jack was eleven, a girl down the street asked if he could come out and ride bikes. Around the block. Without any adults. First of all, it was a really cute girl. So that sent me for a loop. Then it was the whole around-the-block-with-possible-child-molesters-and-potential-drunk-drivers out on the loose. Or at least that was my thought process. But I said, "Yes. Go. Have fun." They rode down the street and I started lacing up my sneakers. Scott looked at me and said, "What are you doing?" I said, "I may just jog after them . . . at a safe distance." He took my hand and said, "You are not going to jog after them. Let him go." Those are such terrible real words. *Let him go.* That is every mom's great fear. The butterflies will fly away. But it is also every mom's great dream. The butterflies will fly away. That is holding on and letting go.

Rooting your children in the knowledge that they have your love and your wisdom to lean on and gently pushing them toward their destiny. Helping them find their wings. Leaning into the leading of God . . . for their own benefit. Opening your hand fully and releasing these precious little big ones to the hands of the One who loves them most of all. There is nothing more beautiful than that.

. . . .

Lord, I am scared to let go and let these sweet kids grow up.
But I want to release them to Your hands
and the destiny that You have shaped for them.
Root them in Your love and give them wings. Amen.

A Good Queen
Keeps *No Record*
of Being Wronged.

CHAPTER 39

Messing Up

*If we confess our sins, he is faithful and just
and will forgive us our sins and purify us
from all unrighteousness.*

1 John 1:9

I AM ALWAYS SUPER-SURPRISED when my kids lie to me. Because I can always tell they are lying. They have some pretty specific lying tells. One child's eyes almost roll completely into the back of his head, mid-lie. I just ask him, "Did you know that your eyes are rolling back in your head because you are lying?" "I am not lying." Another complete eye roll. Another child talks at the speed of light. As if to try to confuse me with his fast talking. The third keeps his eye line at a complete diagonal, as if talking to my left elbow will help me believe his story more. It doesn't.

I should not be surprised that my children lie. I was a HUGE liar as a child. I also stole things. And lied about the things I stole. I was telling the boys this the other day. How I had stolen a toy from our church nursery. Being a pastor's kid, the places I could steal from were limited. Will then proceeded to tell me something he had done recently that was not on the up-and-up. I said, "What in the world! We are going to have to talk about that." He said, "Mom! I thought we were bonding over bad things we had done. I wouldn't have told you if I thought I would get in trouble!"

We shouldn't really be surprised that our kids disobey. That they cheat or lie or steal. Because they are like us. Broken. Human. Trying to be the best that they can be but all the while wanting what they want. Self-control takes lots of years of practice. It also takes the presence of the Holy Spirit deep at work in our hearts. Turning a blind eye to our children's struggles doesn't really help anyone. Pretending that they will never sin or have difficulties with being honest or somehow be miraculously perfect when we ourselves aren't is an exercise in denial. I should know. I wallow in it regularly. But I have also started praying, "God, if there is something that my boys are doing that isn't good or right, bring it into the light." I have told the boys this. I think it freaked them out. It is not that I take joy in finding out their sins. But I know that sin left in the dark does its worst work destroying small hearts from the inside out. I know this because I have experienced it myself. But I also know that as moms, we have the opportunity to bring discipline, boundaries, and healing grace to our kids. Just like we have experienced ourselves.

My friend Lora told me once, "We would love for our kids to make their big mistakes while they are at home with us. So that we can be there to walk them through it and help pick up the pieces." That would be the opposite of me clenching my fists at my side thinking, *Dear God, please don't ever let them make a dumb decision or a mistake or get hurt.* I can tend to be unrealistic. There is freedom in realizing that being a mom and raising people is imperfect work. Always. That mistakes will be made by both you and your child. And the beauty of being a mom is that when your child makes a mistake, you can say, "Oh man! I have been there. I am a genius at mess-ups. But let me show you how to get out of this mess." It is and was what Jesus does for you. He doesn't leave you in your mess. He always shows you the way out with His love and forgiveness. And isn't it a beautiful thing, that you get to do the same?

• • • • • • • • • • • • • • • • • •

Lord, thank You for the revealing light of Your love.
Show me how to walk in that light. Pour out Your grace
and mercy and truth on my children. Bring them close to You.
Forgive them. Hold them close. Amen.

I am *not afraid*.
I was born to do this.

Joan of Arc

CHAPTER 40

Fighting Fear

When I am afraid, I put my trust in you.

Psalm 56:3

WHEN JACK WAS two years old and Will was just a newborn, Scott and I lived with my parents in Virginia for a year. They owned an adorable cottage on a busy street with a driveway that ran down a small hill to a larger parking area. One day, after my mom and I had gone to the grocery store together, I was unloading the little ones from the car. I took Jack out and set him down next to me. Then I reached back inside to unhook Will's infant car seat from the base, and turned to find that Jack was no longer next to me. I called, "Jack?" And I heard his small voice from the top of the driveway. A good fifty feet away from me. I passed off Will to my mom and ran around the side of the car. Jack was standing on the sidewalk, mere feet away from the busy traffic rushing by the house.

I cannot describe the fear that enveloped me in that moment. I tried to be calm. I walked quickly up the driveway to Jack. "Jack, Mom needs you to come hold my hand." I didn't want to freak him out and send my two-year-old bolting into oncoming traffic. He didn't say anything. He didn't move. He just watched me walk toward him, hands out. When I reached him, I grabbed him up in my arms and cried into his neck. He was so precious. The thought that I could have lost him in that split second left me undone.

Here I am all these years later. Jack is a teenager. And there are moments when I look at him and still feel like he is standing on that sidewalk, inches away from danger, far from my arms. Being a mom is scary. Anytime you love that much, you have so much to lose. Our mommy hearts long to protect our children at all costs. Sometimes we feel like we are watching events and circumstances unfold that we can't control, and we fear for our children. We are paralyzed with that heart-gripping fear that we won't be able to keep them whole and safe, whether it is physically, emotionally, or spiritually. But the truth is, we need to move. Toward the One who holds our children's lives within the sphere of His all-encompassing love.

Life is complicated. There is no way to manage every outcome and ensure that nothing bad will ever happen to the ones whom you love so much. But God is bigger than life. He is outside of time. He is unfathomable in His goodness. He is unmeasurable in His kindness. And His love for our children . . . His children . . . is beyond what we could ever begin to imagine. You are not alone in your hopes of keeping your children safe. You are not alone in your desire to see them grow and flourish and become all that they are destined to be. His perfect love is the only thing that can cast out your fear. Let it overwhelm you and overtake you. Let the greatness of it sweep you up and give you the peace that you need and long for. God will strengthen you and keep you. He will help you in every circumstance. Feel yourself being lifted up and held close even now.

• • • • • • • • • • • • • • • • •

Lord, there are moments when I am paralyzed with fear.
Take my fear and replace it with the knowledge of Your love.
I need to know the steadfastness of Your presence
and Your everlasting mercy. Continue to hold me
and these children whom I love so much. Amen.

Making the decision to have a child—
it is momentous.
It is to decide forever
to have your heart go
walking around outside your body.

Elizabeth Stone

CHAPTER 41

Feeling All the Feels

I pray that out of his glorious riches he may strengthen you
with power through his Spirit in your inner being,
so that Christ may dwell in your hearts through faith.
And I pray that you, being rooted and established in love,
may have power, together with all the Lord's holy people,
to grasp how wide and long and high and deep is the love of
Christ, and to know this love that surpasses knowledge—
that you may be filled to the measure of all the fullness of God.
Ephesians 3:16–19

WHEN JACK WAS IN FIRST GRADE, he was picked to be part of a district-wide spelling bee. To say that we were proud is a bit of an understatement. But Scott and I were newbies when it came to the angst of seeing our child perform in front of others and try to win. Even after a month of spelling practice, the thought of Jack spelling his heart out in front of judges, classmates, and parents almost laid me out. Scott took Jack to the spelling bee, and I dropped my other two boys off at my mother-in-law's house. I arrived midway through the first round. They wouldn't let anyone enter the room while the kids were spelling, so I had my ear pressed to the crack in the door to see if I could hear Jack's voice.

My stomach was churning. At the end of the first round, I made my way in and sat down next to Scott. I was bursting with mother love as Jack spelled his way through four rounds. Then Jack was asked to spell "misled." He paused. And for the love of all that is good and holy, in that slight pause, we died a thousand spelling deaths. And then he, using official spelling bee tactics, asked for the definition. He asked for the word to be repeated. When he said the word "misled," the judges couldn't understand his pronunciation (his *l*'s often sounded like *w*'s). They kept asking him to repeat the word. I could tell that was making him more nervous, and finally, I called out, "He's got it." I think it was against protocol for parents to just yell things out, but we were dying.

Jack spelled it "m-i-s-s-l-e-d" with an extra *s*. The judges said that it was incorrect. Everyone clapped. He came and sat down with us. We showered him with praise and kisses. I could see his little face working so that he wouldn't cry. I said, "Jack, it is okay to be sad. You studied very hard." At this, he burst into tears. So did I. He said, "Mom, I kept thinking, is it one *s* or two *s*'s? One or two?" Stupid *s*. So we survived "our" first competition with a few tears and some consolation doughnuts. The craziest part was that all my hopes were dangling out there, right along with Jack's. His small heart hurting had mine hurting right along with it.

This is what we sign up for as moms. Feeling all the feelings that our children feel, right along with them. You can't separate your heart from theirs. Their joys are yours. Their sorrows are yours. It is not that you are trying to live vicariously through them. It is just that they are a part of you. You care about what they care about. You are rooting them on in all of their growth. It can be painful. But it can also be beautiful.

Your love, your appreciation, your belief in them gives them the roots that they need to flourish. Your compassion and empathy say one thing about you: Your heart beats with love for your kids. God feels all the feelings that we feel, too. It is what He committed to when He walked here on earth. He rejoices with us. And He sorrows with us. Know that in your life-shaping work of motherhood, He is rooting you on with love, with hope, and with joy.

• • • • • • • • • • • • • • • • • •

Lord, thank You for rooting and establishing me in Your love.
Your care for me in every situation is evident.
Help me to love my children in the exact same way. Amen.

I remember my mother's prayers,
and they have always *followed me*.
They have clung to me all my life.

Abraham Lincoln

CHAPTER 42

Praying Heavy

I love the LORD, for he heard my voice;
he heard my cry for mercy. Because he turned his ear to me,
I will call on him as long as I live.

Psalm 116:1–2

WILL IS BECOMING a prayer warrior. Every night before he goes to bed, he covers himself with prayer. He prays that God will bless him and all of his family and friends. He prays against sickness. He especially hates throwing up. He prays that he will have a good rest, and then he settles in for a night of uninterrupted sleep. I send my prayers up along with his. I have prayed a lot of things for my boys over the years. I have prayed for safety, for love to cover them completely, for school, for good friendships, for teachers who will inspire them, and for them to be nice to each other. That last one is a daily prayer.

In the past year, my prayers for my boys have changed. I am praying one prayer: "Jesus, let them know You and love You." That is it. I feel like it covers all the bases. Their safety. Their hopes and dreams. Their hearts. If they can truly know Jesus, recognize His love, and love Him back? Then no matter what difficulty, hardship, or temptation comes their way? They know where to turn.

All of my boys asked Jesus into their hearts when they were little. But asking Jesus into their hearts and finding their way into His are two different things. Getting to know Jesus is a way of life . . . not a onetime choice. If my boys can know Him as their Savior and Friend, if they can learn a little more about His goodness each day and recognize the amazing love that He has for them, then all of my endless hopes and worries for them have found their home. They can rest in the arms of the One who loves them most of all. They can be built up in His wisdom. They can be anchored in His grace. They can find their worth in the abundance of His love.

Whenever I ask my mother-in-law to pray for the boys about something, she says, "We're praying heavy." I love that thought. She is sending up weighty prayers to the One who loves my boys most of all. Those prayers, the prayers of my parents, of our friends, are a symphony that is tethering my children to hope. I simply want them to know and love their Creator. That is where true life begins and ends. In communion with Jesus. In Him, all things are possible. I don't want them to know Jesus because I know Jesus. I want them to discover, on their own, who He is and the life that He has for them. All they need, both now and in the future, is found in Him. His grace. His forgiveness. His wisdom. His mercy. His purpose. His love. His path.

You tether your children to the God of the Universe with your prayers. You build them up in His truth every time you read Scripture over them. Bedtime prayers aren't just simple words to be repeated. They are battle cries. They echo throughout eternity, surrounding your child with the hope and truth that the God who created them loves them and wants to know them. Before you ever saw your beautiful child's face, it was seen by the One who loves him most of all. Before you spoke her name, it was etched on the palm of the Creator of the universe. You are a powerful link from your child to the One who breathed life into him or her. Your prayers are foundational. God hears the prayers of your mother's heart. And He is shouting back across, "Keep going! I'm listening!"

• • • • • • • • • • • • • • • • •

*Lord, You know the desires of my heart. You know that,
more than anything, I want my child to know You.
Please keep them close to Your heart.
Don't let them get away from Your love.
Hem them in on all sides with Your protection and grace.
Hold them close until they meet You face-to-face. Amen.*

My Heavy Prayers for My Child

_____

_____

_____

_____

_____

_____

_____

_____

_____

_____

_____

_____

_____

_____

_____

_____

_____

It is okay to *pray*
while you do the dishes.
Life can be *busy*
with babies and children.

Traci Foth

CHAPTER 43

Balancing Life

There is a time for everything,
and a season for every activity under the heavens.

Ecclesiastes 3:1

MY SON ADDISON came in the other day and said, "Are you writing AGAIN?" Now that the boys are out of school, they actually see that I have to work. That I don't just sit around and eat bonbons and watch movies while they are in class. I said, "Yes, I am writing again." "When will you be done?" "In a couple of hours." "Awwwwwrghhh." This is the sound that came out of his body. Clearly, me writing for a couple of hours was not going to work for him. I looked at him and said, "I'm sorry that it is hard for you when I work. But you know that if I didn't have this job, I would have to have another job, right?" He looked at me in confusion. "Why?" "Because you like to eat food." "So?" "How do you think that Dad and I pay for the food that you love to eat so much?" He was quiet, and then he said, "It's just that you work *so much.*"

This has been a particularly busy writing season for me. Both a blessing and a curse. As a writer, you never know when your next gig is going to come, so the frequent jobs have been a blessing. But as a mom, juggling life with three boys, connecting with my husband, running the church's kids program, trying to get meals on the table, and keeping the children in pants that don't look like knickers? Not an easy task. The last eight months haven't been pretty. And Addison is here to let me know it. My cousin Gretchen calls her life with her four boys "The Circus." Welcome to my circus.

I have never even once in my life had a mom come up to me and say, "The one thing I can say about my life is that it is completely balanced in all aspects." I have had quite a few moms say to me, "I can't remember my name anymore," or "We eat out five nights a week because my brains are exhausted." All of us moms have our own version of the circus. Trying to balance the many arenas of our lives can be overwhelming. Some days we do great. Other days? Not so much. Whether you are a stay-at-home mom, a work-from-home mom, or a work-outside-of-the-home mom, trying to run "the circus" of your life smoothly can feel impossible.

I was talking about this to my mom once and I told her, "Whoever it was that said you can have it all was lying." She laughed and said, "You can have it all. Just not all at once. There are different seasons of your life when different pieces will fall into place." Hearing that let me breathe.

Whatever season of motherhood you are in, your circus will look different. You may not be able to have a clean house while you have children at home. Breathe. But you can have more fun and more hugs with children at home. Breathe. You may not be able to put a three-course meal on the table every night while you have a full-time job. Breathe. But your job is buying the takeout Chinese that is feeding your family. Breathe. You may not be able to teach the class at church that you have been asked to teach. Breathe. But you are teaching your little ones every day about the God of the Universe who loves them most of all. Breathe.

You may be the queen, but there is only one Person who brings perfect order to the universe. His name is Jesus. The rest of us won't actually see it come to pass in our lives until heaven. That is okay. Jesus is with you in the mess of your daily life. He is shouting with joy with all that you are accomplishing. He is cheering you on as you love your kids in all the different ways that you love them. With your words. With your kisses. With your work. With your discipline. And when you are exhausted from all of the circus-ing, He is standing there with arms open wide, inviting you to rest in Him. I think you should.

• • • • • • • • • • • • • • • •

Lord, You see the circus of my life. Help me focus on the things that are important and let go of everything else. I am ready to rest in You. Amen.

When all else fails . . .
sweep the leg.

Cheri Bondonno

CHAPTER 44

Protecting Little People

"Because he loves me," says the LORD, "I will rescue him;
I will protect him, for he acknowledges my name.
He will call on me, and I will answer him; I will be with him
in trouble, I will deliver him and honor him. With long life
I will satisfy him and show him my salvation."

Psalm 91:14–16

I WOULD HAVE TO SAY that I am a lover, not a fighter. Unless you want to try to do something to one of my kids. And then I will have to take you down. This shouldn't be a surprise. Everyone knows that you don't mess with Mama. That protective instinct is pretty strong. When one of my boys was being bullied at school during recess, he begged me not to talk to the principal. He was in tears. I told him, "If I don't talk to the principal about this, I am not being a good mom." Then I said, "I could come to school at recess and hang out on the playground. I would make sure no one bullied you. EVER." This actually made him cry harder. The thought of me showing up at recess almost sent him over the edge. But let's be honest. Moms don't play around.

We moms take our jobs seriously. My sister-in-law, Cheri, once gave a warning to her son, Brian, and his youth group friends when they were planning an outing. "Don't do anything crazy. I will sweep the leg." Cheri is five feet tall. Brian is six-foot-one. He looked at his friends and said, "She is not kidding. She will do it." Cheri wanted Brian and his friends to be safe at all costs. Putting a little karate smackdown fear into their teenage hearts was an incentive to keep them on a good path. As far as I know, no one has ever messed with her or her kids. I know I haven't.

It is not just physical safety that we moms are concerned about. We want to protect our children mentally, spiritually, and emotionally, too. When my boys were little, I took them to the playground at a nearby school. There were some teenagers using the blacktop to ride their bikes. One of the boys stopped near the play area to talk on the phone. He was using some colorful language. My head snapped around. I looked him in the eye and said, sternly, "Watch your mouth! There are kids here." His eyes went wide. He turned bright red, and he said, "I'm sorry." I think he probably turned red because I reminded him of his own mom. We moms all sound a whole lot alike.

There is so much that we are trying to protect our kids from. Crazy talk. Crazy choices. Crazy friends. Sometimes the threat of sweeping the leg isn't enough. Sometimes the prospect of trying to protect our kids from a broken world leaves us feeling broken. Because we know that no matter how hard we try, it is an impossibility. As a mom, that can feel unbearable. We feel like we have failed when our children are lost and hurting. But if we are being honest with ourselves, there is no way for our children to be members of humanity without feeling the pain of being human.

But this is the thing. All hope is not lost. In the darkest spaces, in the hurting, jagged places of their childhood, teenager-hood, and adulthood, there is One who heals, who redeems, who restores, who breathes life and hope. God is the true Protector. Your child is the apple of His eye. His heart beats with love for him . . . for her. Whatever pain, whatever heartache that your child encounters, there is healing to be found for them and for you, in the wideness of God's embrace. He is writing the story of their lives. He is with them in the heights of joy and in the depths of sorrow, and He is holding them in His arms. Even now.

• • • • • • • • • • • • • • • • • •

Lord, You are the protector of my children.
Surround them with Your presence. Help them to know
the sound of Your voice. Comfort them when they are hurting.
Heal their wounds . . . and mine. Amen.

These *are*
the good old days.

Erica Foth Clements

CHAPTER 45

Remembering the Good

The life of mortals is like grass, they flourish like a flower
of the field; the wind blows over it and it is gone,
and its place remembers it no more. But from everlasting
to everlasting the LORD's love is with those who fear him,
and his righteousness with their children's children—
with those who keep his covenant
and remember to obey his precepts.

Psalm 103:15–18

MY SISTER ERICA said something to me a few years back that has stuck with me as I march forward into the teenage years of mothering. She said that she and her husband, Van, would look at each other when their four kids, ages eleven and under, were crammed into their car, poking their fingers into each other's ears, arguing over whose side of the line was whose, and say, "These are the good old days." The very full, very wild, very crazy good old days. These are the days of sleepless nights and high laughter. The days when little bodies press into your side for a hug and whisper love words in your ears. These are the days when one child decides that flushing toothbrushes down the toilet should be a thing and another decides that they hate chicken even though chicken has been on the menu for the last seven years. These are the good old days.

As my kids have gotten older, as they have moved from diapers to preschool, elementary into junior high, and then taken the leap from middle school to high school, we are blazing a fast trail. I felt those golden days of young childhood slipping through my fingers like sand. The boys' voices are changing, and they are wearing bigger shoes than I am. But Scott and I still look at each other and say, "Hey. These are the good old days." The days when the kids make us laugh with their own unique senses of humor. The days when decisions weigh more and challenges are stretching their minds and hearts. The days when they seem to grow an inch in a week and grow quiet about the things that matter most to them. These are the days when I press into their tall frames for a hug and whisper, "I really love you, kid." These are the good old days.

The truth is that this path of motherhood . . . it starts out slow, then starts to pick up speed. By the time you hit the school years, it takes off like a comet at breakneck speed. It is hard to hold on to a comet. You are trying to shape and mold and encourage these little ones, and all the while, you are flying through the universe at the speed of light. It is easy to get distracted by life, but taking a breath and shouting out loud, "These are the good old days!" lets you take a moment to recognize that goodness that surrounds you. Whether you are holding your first baby in your arms or kissing your college freshman all over her precious face as you drop her off at her dorm, every moment, every triumph, every hurdle that you jump over is something to be acknowledged.

God's goodness is surrounding you at every turn. His love and faithfulness are the foundation of this mom life. Even on the most difficult days. Even when life is overwhelming and bills are piling up and your children are overly curious. Holding your child in your arms, even for one wiggly moment, can remind you that you are blessed. With life. With hope. With a new crack at a new day tomorrow. Your teething baby who is crying her head off, your smelly car packed with grubby kids, your teenager caught up in the throes of hormonal change puts you smack-dab in the middle of the good old days. There will never be another day like today. This mom moment is yours to grab and cherish. Grab on to the One who loves you the most. Tether yourself to His faithfulness. And hold on for the ride of your life.

• • • • • • • • • • • • • • • • • •

Lord, thank You for Your all-encompassing love.
Remind me once again that this season of motherhood
is fleeting. Help me to enjoy every moment
that You have given me with these little ones. Amen.

You don't choose your family.
They are *God's gift* to you,
as you are to them.

Desmond Tutu

CHAPTER 46

The Best Gift

Your eyes saw my unformed body; all the days ordained for me were written in your book before one of them came to be.

Psalm 139:16

MY SON WILL ADORES his cousin Lily. She is seven months old and lights up the world with her smile. When she is in the room, Will only has eyes for her. He holds her. Plays with her. Makes her laugh. He bounces her on his knees and tickles her. Now that summer is here, Will wants to visit her. Every day. Will has a thing for babies in general. He begs me to work in the nursery at church so that he can play with all the little ones. He has a special connection with them. They love him, and he loves them back.

When we were talking about what Will wanted to do when he grew up, he thought about it for a minute and said, "I would like to be a stay-at-home dad. And take care of my kids." That made me want to cry a little. I love his heart for kids. Will would be a fantastic stay-at-home dad. His care for children is evident even now. The desire that Will has to be a dad is ingrained in his DNA. I completely get it. When I was growing up, one of my greatest heart's desires was to be a mom. I could hardly stand looking at cute babies without getting my hands on them. I loved the smell and feel of all my baby cousins and would ask to hold them constantly. Scott loves babies, too. He has the ability to connect with them through baby talk and funny faces. Babies can't take their eyes off of him.

The gift of parenthood . . . the gift of motherhood . . . is something that changes you forever. The days when I was crowned Queen of the Universe, mom of three boys? Best days ever. The first time I held Jack in my arms I wept. Scott wept. We blubbered together. For the beauty of it. For the sheer enormity of love that engulfed us when we saw this sweet little boy. The same thing happened when we met Will and Addison for the first time, in all their newness. We touched their tiny faces. We marveled at their perfect hands with dimpled knuckles and miniature nails. We adored them. Every part of them was perfection. Their perfection came simply from the fact that these babies were ours. I had never felt the joy that I felt in those moments. These little ones were the best gifts I had ever been given. The opportunity to be their mom was something I had longed for, and now here I was, getting to live out that dream.

What I have realized in these last fifteen years is that this gift of being able to love and care for these boys requires a daily relinquishment on my part. Because even though I look at them and say, "These are my boys and I am their mom," there is the unspoken truth that they were never truly mine to keep. They are God's boys, on loan to Scott and me, to love and nurture and grow up to manhood. As their mom, I have the choice of how I steward the gift of these amazing boys in my life. I get to invest in them. Share them with others. Encourage them to be brave and honest. Tell them and show them how much God loves them. And then I get to place them back into His hands. The hands that knit their small hearts together and formed their bodies and shaped their souls. This is holy work that you and I are doing as moms.

Motherhood really is a gift. In this moment. In this space. You have in your arms one whom God adores. He has trusted you with the care of His children. And each day, as you love them and grow them, you get to choose to place them back in His care. These little people are part of who you are, but they are also on their own trajectory of growing and becoming. You are stewarding the years, investing, nurturing, and praying over these children. But ultimately they are His little ones. And you get the opportunity to relinquish this amazing gift back into His care each day, with every breath, saying, "God, Your will be done."

• • • • • • • • • • • • • •

Lord, thank You for the gift of my child.
Thank You for the opportunity to grow and love
and shape his life. Thank You for the way
that being a mom has changed me.
I give this child back into Your care today.
Surround them with Your grace and presence. Amen.

A Good Queen
Doesn't Demand
Her Own Way.

CHAPTER 47

Needing Jesus

*I waited patiently for the LORD; he turned to me
and heard my cry. He lifted me out of the slimy pit,
out of the mud and mire; he set my feet on a rock
and gave me a firm place to stand.*

Psalm 40:1–2

I CALLED MY SISTER ERICA the other day and told her, "I know that I am supposed to know what I am doing as a mom. Don't tell my kids, but I don't have a clue." She just laughed and said, "Welcome to the club." She has four kids, two of whom are married. She has already blazed the parenting trail before me. It was good to know I am not alone in feeling like I have no idea how to parent my own children. Motherhood is an adventure in the unknown—doing so many things that I have never done before.

When my kids were babies, I had two goals: keep them alive and get as much sleep as possible. But these days I have to worry about much more than just keeping them alive. With the craziness of the world, the onslaught of technology, and the wildness of trying to launch young people into life with a solid foundation of truth, I often feel like I am at a loss. I told Jack, our oldest, "I am sorry, buddy, but we are trying it all out on you. Hopefully, by the time we get to your youngest brother, we will be able to figure it out." He looked at me with a certain degree of sadness and said, "I know, Mom. I'm the experiment." He felt it before I ever told him.

I have ideas and hopes and dreams for my boys. But what I really want for them is the life that God has designed for them. I mess up. I falter. I make mistakes. But luckily for me, there is Someone who knows everything about everything. There is nothing that surprises Him or catches Him off guard. He is not scared about the future or stumped about the past. He is here right now, with me in the middle of my mothering. He knows that my brain is tired after years of sleep-deprivation. He knows that my creativity and resilience can wear thin. He knows that I don't have all the answers to their questions. He knows that I am broken and finite and imperfect in almost every way. But He also knows that I am longing for His wisdom. And He is thrilled. Because His resources are limitless. His knowledge is infinite. His creativity is exponential. And He wants to share them all with me. All He is waiting for me to say is, "I need You. Please help me." That is the truth of it. I need Jesus. You need Jesus.

There are mothering moments that will break you right down and make you wonder if maybe you signed up for the wrong life. There are times when your heart will be cracked with worry over the path that your kids seem to be taking. There will be days lost to confusion as you are trying to figure out how to best love your child. Should you flood them with grace? Should you forgive them and give them a second chance? Should you discipline them? Should you fall on your face and ask the God of the Universe to intervene because you have absolutely no clue what to do next? Yes, yes, yes, and especially, whatever you decide, a ginormous yes to the last question.

God didn't fling you out into the mom ether and say, "Figure it out. Good luck." He sent His Son, Jesus, to make a way for you to have a relationship with Him. He wants to share all of who He is with you on your mothering journey. His mercy. His comfort. His peace. His incomprehensible wisdom. He longs to get in on the daily-ness of your decisions and your deepest conundrums. He has so much truth and grace that He longs to pour into you with His Word. He will supply your every need. And that is good to know.

• • • • • • • • • • • • • • • • • •

Lord, I need You. I need Your wisdom and presence in my life as I raise my child. I need Your strength to lift me up and hold me. Thank You for Your endless love for both me and my child. Amen.

Bless your ever loving
little *heart.*

Stanley Murphy

CHAPTER 48

Blessing You

No power in the sky above or in the earth below—
indeed, nothing in all creation will ever be able
to separate us from the love of God
that is revealed in Christ Jesus our Lord.

Romans 8:39 NLT

I HAVE A FRIEND who will look at you and say, "Well, bless your heart," when you are going through a difficult time. One year she was "blessing my heart" regularly. The year after I had my third son, Addison, I was sent spiraling into the depths of postpartum depression. I was completely unprepared for the chaos of life with three boys aged five and under. I was on a wild ride of sleep-deprivation and anxiety. I was constantly anxious, worried, tired, and overwhelmed. I couldn't get a grip on my thoughts, or my emotions for that matter. I thought I would never be able to dig myself out of the pit of despair that I was in. I felt alone. I felt like a loser mom. And I felt like it would never change.

I would look at my boys and think, *I know that I am blessed to have these three healthy boys. What is wrong with me?* I felt like since I had birthed people, that somehow mothering would not be difficult. That every day would be filled with a golden glow and that I should be able to figure out how to nurture, love, and care for these three little ones, even though I couldn't make it through the day without collapsing into tears. Those were some dark days. It was the love of family and the wise words of a good counselor that got me moving toward the light.

I learned some truths during that time that I still cling to:

It is okay to cry.

What I feel and what is actually true
can be two different things.

A good counselor can be an angel sent from God.

Sleep is worth more than gold.

Friends and family will hold you together
when you cannot do it yourself.

There is no golden glow of motherhood.

Being blessed doesn't mean that everything
feels good all the time.

Life can be both hard and beautiful.

And most importantly, there may be some seasons of darkness that we walk through as moms, but God does not leave us there, forsaken and alone.

God comes for us with all of His love.

No matter what season you are facing, whatever worries or fears or dark place that you are in at this moment, God is coming for you with the deepness and wideness and greatness of His love. He never leaves you in the dark. The light can seem a long time coming. It can seem like you will never get a break, and you wonder how in the world you can take care of little people when you are not sure how to take care of yourself. But He is on His way.

God is running all-out—full of peace and hope and goodness. He is flinging open the doors of truth, setting captives free, lighting up the dark. And He is headed your way. He brings His light with the people whom He has placed in your life. He brings it with the comfort of His Holy Spirit and the truth of His Word. He brings it with the care and counsel of those who surround you. No matter what you may be feeling, you can know that you are not alone. Ever.

• • • • • • • • • • • • • • • • • • •

Lord, shine Your light into my life.
Remind me that I am not alone and that no matter what,
You are coming for me. Keep me in Your perfect peace
and built up with Your truth. I love You. Amen.

A Good Queen
Rejoices
When the Truth
Wins Out.

• • • • • • • • • • • •

CHAPTER 49

Giving Up

Blessed is the one who perseveres under trial because,
having stood the test, that person will receive the crown of life
that the Lord has promised to those who love him.

James 1:12

THE SCIENCE FAIR is just about my least-favorite school project ever. I didn't even like the science fair when I was a child, so to have to help my children with their projects seems like a highly ironic form of torture. Since we live near Silicon Valley, the pulsing heart of technology and software development, you can imagine the types of projects that come into the school. Awe-inspiring experiments. Beautiful displays. Cutting-edge thoughts and ideas neatly graphed on pie charts and such. Some projects come in looking like they were put together by NASA. No one ever looks at my kids' projects and thinks that. They think, *Oh, these parents really let their kids go for it . . . on their own . . . good for them?*

The week before the boys' projects were due, I was talking to one of the dads who was helping his kids with their projects. He told me, "We are trying to show how the tectonic plates of the earth shift when there is an earthquake." I said, "That is amazing. Wow." "What projects are your kids doing?" I cleared my throat. "My boys are trying to figure out

How Long Before M&M's Really Melt in Your Hands? and How Big Can You Grow a Gummy Worm?" The dad said, "That is great!" He was super-supportive of our clearly world-changing work in the field of candy. I was on the verge of asking him whether he would like to adopt my children and do their projects for them.

I think it was around the fourth go at Will's experiment of melting M&M's in the microwave that I truly lost my mind. I was trying to convince him of the necessity that he needed to use the same color M&M's for the experiment, since different colors of dye could melt at different speeds. The scientific method is an actual . . . method. You have to be precise in your measurements. You need to narrow down the variables to get the best scientific findings. I am Madame Curie when it comes to chocolate. He looked at me and said, "Mom . . . just let me do my project." I think I said something encouraging like, "Whatever. You are on your own."

There are so many moments in momhood that invite despair. It is easy to want to throw up your hands and cry, "Uncle!" Toddler tantrums. Defiant behavior. Sibling violence. General disobedience. Struggles with homework. The never-ending war of determining how much screen time is too much screen time. The science fair. The list goes on and on. We want to say, "I give up," or "I am done," or "You are on your own." Discouragement can flood in. We feel like we aren't making any headway. What difference does it all make anyway?

The enemy would love for your mind to be full of doubt

and discouragement on this journey of mothering. He would love for you to put in less effort and care less about these little ones. But the truth is that you are on the winning team. The truth is that your heavenly Father is on your side. The truth is that He is in control in every possible way and in every possible circumstance. The truth is that He values you. And the truth is what matters. God sees your heart for your children and the passion that He has given you for them. He knows that you can grow weary with all the work. *All the work.* And He sees the secret fears that lace your thoughts, the ones that say, *I don't think I am doing this right*, and *I am so scared that I am failing.* And He is shouting out across the miles, "Don't be discouraged. Don't be afraid. Don't give up. *Keep going.* I am right here. I won't ever leave you alone. I will give you all the strength you need!" So, be encouraged. Open your heart and let Him fill you up with His grace and His strength.

• • • • • • • • • • • • • • • • •

Lord, thank You that You don't ever give up on me.
I need Your strength to fill me up from head to toe.
Flood me with Your courage and help me persevere. Amen.

Nothing ever comes to one,
that is *worth having,*
except as a result
of *hard work.*

Booker T. Washington

CHAPTER 50

Knowing Him

My sheep listen to my voice;
I know them, and they follow me.

John 10:27

THE OTHER NIGHT my son Addison climbed into bed next to me. At ten, he is the only one who still thinks snuggling with Mom is cool. I mostly get high fives and side hugs from my older boys. But Addie pressed his shoulder against mine, and we began to talk. I loved the closeness of him. The sound of his voice. The way that he laughs when he thinks something is funny. He is growing and changing before my eyes. He is a deep thinker and a pray-er. I love the way that his mind mulls things over. We talked about all kinds of things . . . life, summer, swimming lessons (which he does not want), video games (which he does want), and then we talked about Jesus.

I asked Addie, "Have you ever heard God's voice?" He shook his head. "No, Mom, have you ever heard Him?" I said, "I have never heard Him talk to me out loud. But I have had thoughts that I know are His thoughts . . . that sound like His truth. When I talk to Him, I have felt His presence." "I haven't ever felt anything." I told Addie, "That's okay. Knowing God isn't all about feelings. And people ex- perience Him in all sorts of different ways." "Yeah." As we talked, it wasn't like I was a mom teaching her son about God. It was more like two pilgrims on a journey sharing their experiences. Wanting to find the truth, to know what God has for them. Because I am still learning and Addie is still learning. It was a shift in our relationship, subtle and honest. I shared my heart with him. He shared his with me.

I have so many hopes for Addison. My biggest hope is that he will know Jesus in his own right. I long for the power of God and the truth of who He is to penetrate Addie's heart. But the truth of the matter is, I want those things for myself, too. I don't have all the answers. I still make mistakes and have to ask for forgiveness on a daily basis. I still struggle to let go of my perfectionist ways and comprehend His path for me. Every day I see my own brokenness and need to step into the wide river of grace for healing. This journey of loving Jesus and loving kids, it isn't easy. But then, nothing that is truly good and worth living for ever is.

You are on a journey of loving Jesus and loving your kids. You probably don't have it all figured out. If you do, please give a heads-up to the rest of us. We could use your wisdom. But as you follow Jesus, you are exposing your kids to His love, to His mercy, and to His life-altering truths. Your life being shaped by Jesus is shaping theirs. Motherhood is a life calling. It is good hard work that somehow seems to get both harder and better as the years go by. Being queen isn't easy . . . but it is worth it.

Following Jesus and loving your kids? It is a day-by-day journey, year in and year out. As you grow and as they grow, you are held in a place of love by your heavenly Father. He is rooting for you to know Him. He doesn't expect you to get everything right. He just wants you to keep trying. He wants to reveal all of His glory and power in your life. In your children's lives. And the opportunity to know Him better each day? That is a truly glorious thing.

• • • • • • • • • • • • • • • • • •

Lord, following You is worth everything that I have.
I want to know You more. I want my kids to know
Your love and forgiveness. Thank You for this journey
that You have put me on. Amen.

I love *you* the most!

Ruth Foth

CHAPTER 51

Loving You

He answered, "'Love the Lord your God with all your heart and with all your soul and with all your strength and with all your mind'; and, 'Love your neighbor as yourself.'"

Luke 10:27

YEARS AGO, I WAS at my sister Jenny's baby shower for her son, Drew. I had the chance to sit near a good friend of both of ours. Her kids were in high school and going into college, while mine were just heading into elementary school. She was and is one of those wise, calm women (the opposite of me) whom I longed to learn from as a young mom. When she talks, I listen. We got a chance to laugh together and we ate cake. Then she said something that I had never thought of before. She said, "I have been learning how to love myself better. When Jesus talks about loving your neighbor, He says, 'Love your neighbor like you love yourself.' If you don't love yourself, it is really hard to love your neighbor." If you don't love yourself, how can you love anyone else? I don't know.

It made me think of the love chapter, 1 Corinthians 13, and all the different attributes of love. Here I am, walking out the path of being the good queen . . . loving my kids in a million different ways, but do I treat myself with the same care? Do I really love myself?

Love is patient.
Love is not boastful.
Love is kind.
Love is not jealous.
Love is not proud.
Love is not rude.
Love doesn't demand its own way.
Love is not irritable.
Love keeps no record of being wronged.
Love doesn't rejoice about injustice, but rejoices
    whenever the truth wins out.
Love never gives up.
Love never loses faith.
Love is always hopeful.
Love endures through every circumstance.

Love has so many different facets to it. It always brings healing and hope. Years later, here I am still thinking about this conversation about loving myself. In this good hard work of mothering, it is easy to be very hard on oneself. There are so many ways not to be the mothers that we long and hope to be. We tend to give ourselves very little grace when we disappoint ourselves as moms. It is easy to forget that we are still . . . becoming. We are changing every day. We are being shaped by our circumstances, our hopes, and our relationships. The relationship that is shaping us the most is the one we have with Jesus. And He is relentless in His love toward us. He sees us as we are. And He knows who we are destined to become. He encompasses us in His loving-kindness, filling us with strength for each mothering day. And He is telling us He would appreciate it if we loved ourselves, for our own benefit and for the benefit of our neighbors. Especially those little neighbors who live right under our feet all day.

What would a mom day look like for you if you truly loved yourself? If you were kind and generous and protective toward . . . you? If you forgave yourself and trusted yourself and weren't angry with yourself? What would it feel like if you recognized your own perpetual state of "becoming" and kept marching on with patience and hope and perseverance? It might give you some space to breathe. It might fill you with overflowing joy that would pour out onto those little ones around you. It might look like a new kind of day, when you gave yourself space to grow and learn and just be. That is how love works.

Jesus loves you most of all. He loves who you are becoming as you hang out with Him and hang out with the kids He gave you. He gave those little ones to you so that you could have a small glimpse of the enormous amount of love and affection that He has for you. It is just about time for you to revel in it. And to love yourself like He loves you.

• • • • • • • • • • • • • • • • • •

*Lord, thank You for Your great, great love. Show me how
to love myself so that I can love these little ones.
Bring the truth of Your love into every corner of my life
so that it spills up and out and over to everyone I know. Amen.*

To be a queen
of a household
is a *powerful* thing.

Jill Scott

CHAPTER 52

Queen for Life

"His master replied, 'Well done, good and faithful servant!
You have been faithful with a few things;
I will put you in charge of many things.
Come and share your master's happiness!'"

Matthew 25:23

I WAS GETTING MY HAIR CUT yesterday and asked my hairdresser how many kids she had. "I have one." "How old is he?" "He is twenty-seven." "He must be pretty special." "He is still at home with us. His dad and I want to keep him as long as we can. Once he gets married, we know that we won't see him all the time anymore." I almost started weeping into the plastic hair-cutting cape. I so long to keep my boys around as long as I can. I am pretty sure my kids are not going to hang around until they are twenty-seven. But the thought of being separated from them rips my heart right out. This all-encompassing job of mothering, it changes you forever.

Once your heart has been cracked open to love these little people, it never goes back to what it was before. We will always have this space in us, in our lives, reserved for these most precious of people. The ones who have shaped us with their love, with their tiny hands and their full-body hugs. The ones whose smiles light up our lives and whose crazy schemes make us lose our minds. We are who we are because of them.

My mother-in-law, Sandy (whom I call Lola), still comes to church bringing baby pictures of Scott to show our congregation. Scott told her that if she brings his awkward high school pictures, she will no longer be allowed to come to church. But she is so proud of him. She loves him. Every time Scott preaches, Sandy cries. Because of the goodness of it all. Scott was so shy in high school, he never actually went to youth group at church. He told his mom that he would rather die than speak in public. And now here he is, all these years later, shaped by the power of the Holy Spirit, a good man, loving his wife and kids, leading a church, and talking about how good God is. And she can barely stand it . . . because that is her baby up there. All grown up . . . but still. The way that she holds him in her heart is with the same care that she did when he was a tiny, blue-eyed boy with a blond Afro. She still can't get enough of him.

This past month, my mom, Ruth, had open heart surgery to repair her heart valve. All their kids waited with Dad while Mom was in surgery. Four hours of waiting. And then they told us that her heart was beating on its own . . . strong and steady. There were some happy tears and sighs of relief all around. Mom is the love of Dad's life. For us kids, Mom was the center of our universe. She will always be the woman who has loved us most of all. She poured out her life for us every day—making us good food, comforting us when we were sad, holding the pieces of our lives together with her words and wisdom and the steadiness of her presence. We could have told you that her heart beat strong and steady when we were kids. It beat for us. It still does.

The thing is, whether you are twenty-five or seventy-five, you are still Mom . . . Mommy . . . Mother . . . Queen of the Universe. Lover of your children. Prayer warrior. Encourager. Truth teller. Dinner maker. Hand holder. Fighter. Dreamer. Kid launcher. Your place in this world, in the hearts of your children, is powerful. It always will be. You are full of love and grace for them. Your ability to speak hope and truth into their lives, whether they are little or big, is unsurpassed. Your love, however imperfect, has been foundational, launching them into their future. Your prayers tether them to the Most High. Your life is an example of sacrifice and grit, laid out in an overlapping pattern of good hard work and a love so deep it can't be described with mere words. What you have done and what you continue to do is not easy, but it is good. He sees your heart as you chase after Him and long to know Him more. He sees your passion as you love His children with your whole life. And He is shouting across the galaxies and miles, speaking words of light and life over you, saying, "Well done."

. . . .

Lord, thank You for letting me be a mom. Amen.

ABOUT THE AUTHOR

SUSANNA FOTH AUGHTMON is the mother of fifteen-year-old Jack, thirteen-year-old Will, and ten-year-old Addison and the wife of Scott, the lead pastor of Pathway Church, in Redwood City, California. Being a mom of three boys brings her a great amount of joy and also requires a daily infusion of dark chocolate.

She loves connecting with fellow Christ followers through her books and speaking using humor and the focus of how God's grace intersects our daily lives.

Susanna has written *Expectant Blessings*, *Hope Sings*, *All I Need Is Jesus and a Good Pair of Jeans*, *My Bangs Look Good and Other Lies I Tell Myself*, and *I Blame Eve*. She also contributes to Guideposts' *Mornings with Jesus Devotional*.

She blogs regularly about living out this crazy, good life at www.susannaaughtmon.com.

IF YOU ENJOYED THIS BOOK, WILL YOU CONSIDER SHARING THE MESSAGE WITH OTHERS?

Mention the book in a blog post or through Facebook, Twitter, Pinterest, or upload a picture through Instagram.

Recommend this book to those in your small group, book club, workplace, and classes.

Head over to facebook.com/SusannaFothAughtmon, "LIKE" the page, and post a comment as to what you enjoyed the most.

Tweet "I recommend reading #QueenOfTheUniverse by @SusannaAughtmon // @worthypub"

Pick up a copy for someone you know who would be challenged and encouraged by this message.

Write a book review online.

Visit us at worthypublishing.com

twitter.com/worthypub

worthypub.tumblr.com

facebook.com/worthypublishing

pinterest.com/worthypub

instagram.com/worthypub

youtube.com/worthypublishing